"That love is inexhaustible,
you will be there"

forever

_____

_____

_____

_____

_____

THIS BOOK
Belongs to

_____

_____

Visit Our Author Page At
amazon.com

Scan me

Black Rose PRESS HOUSE

MIXED TATTOO COLORING BOOK

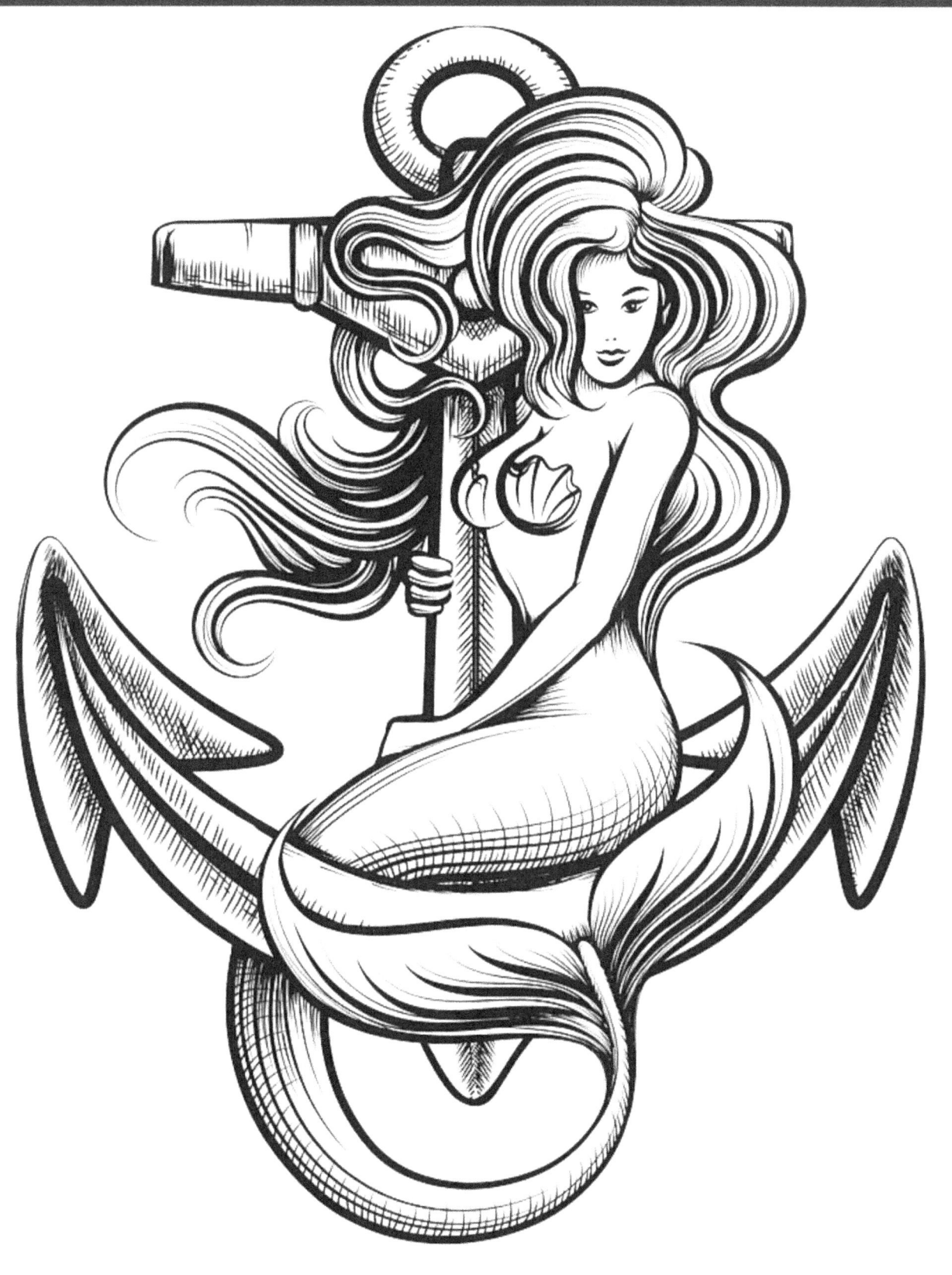

MIXED TATTOO COLORING BOOK

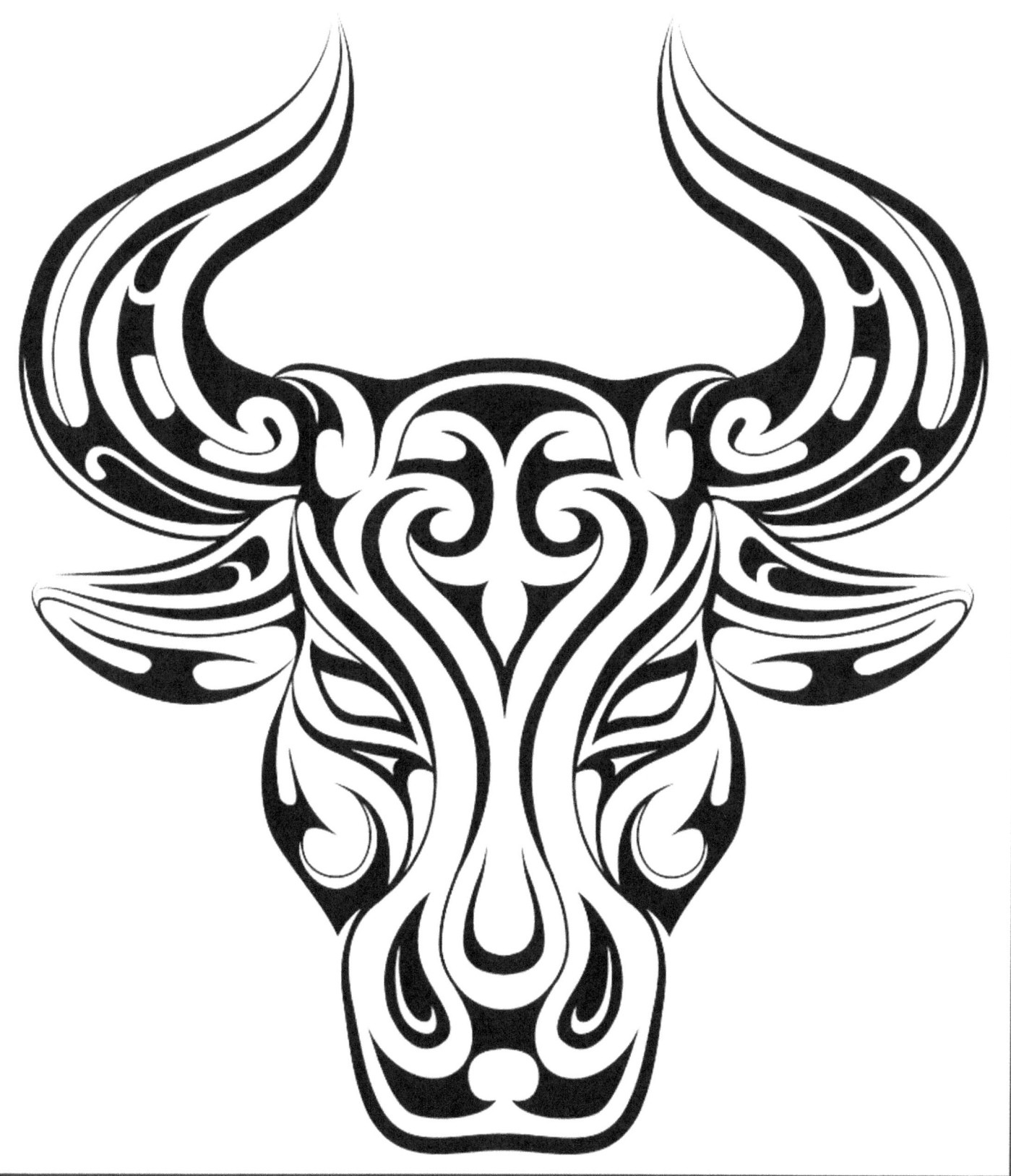

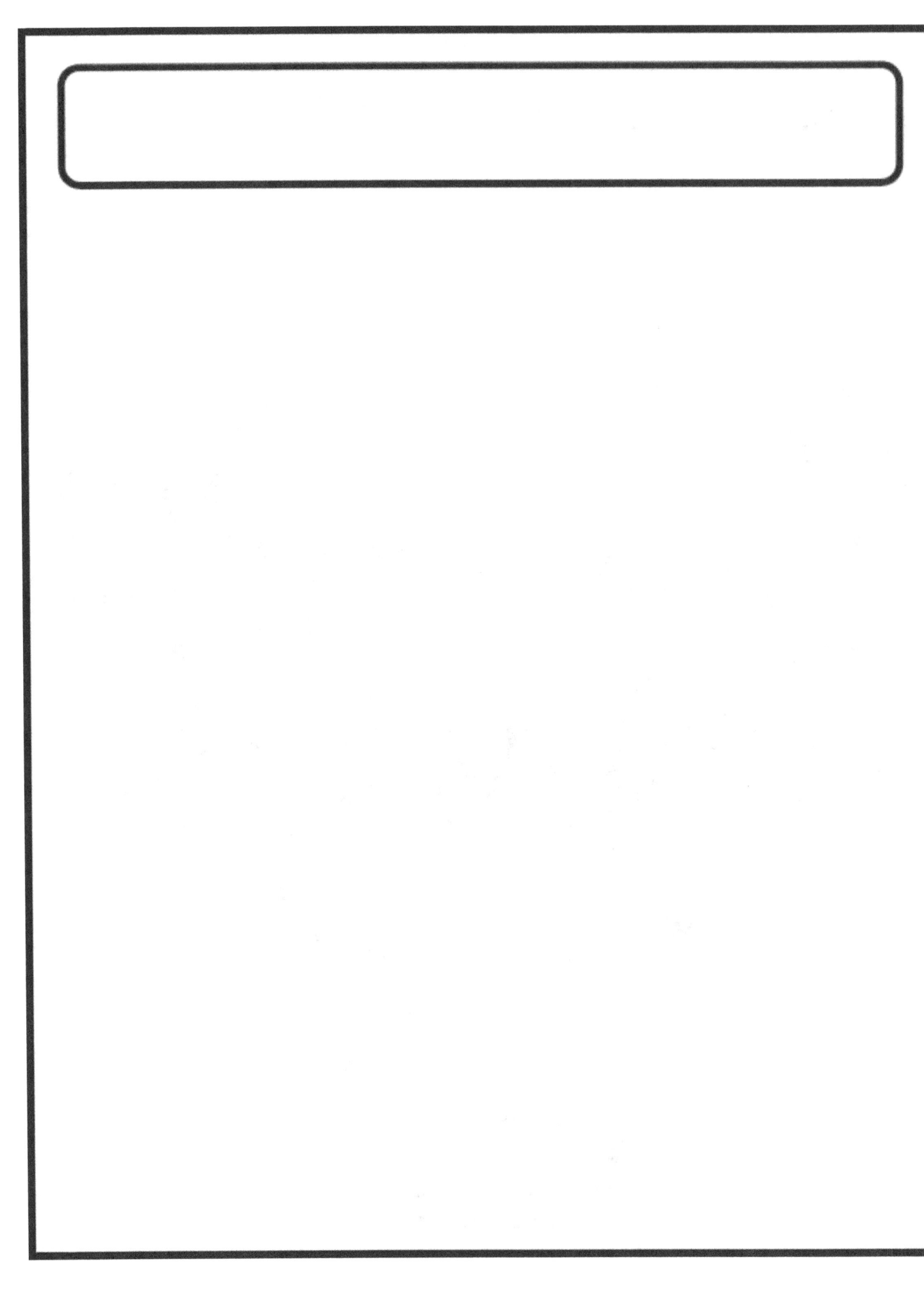

MIXED TATTOO COLORING BOOK

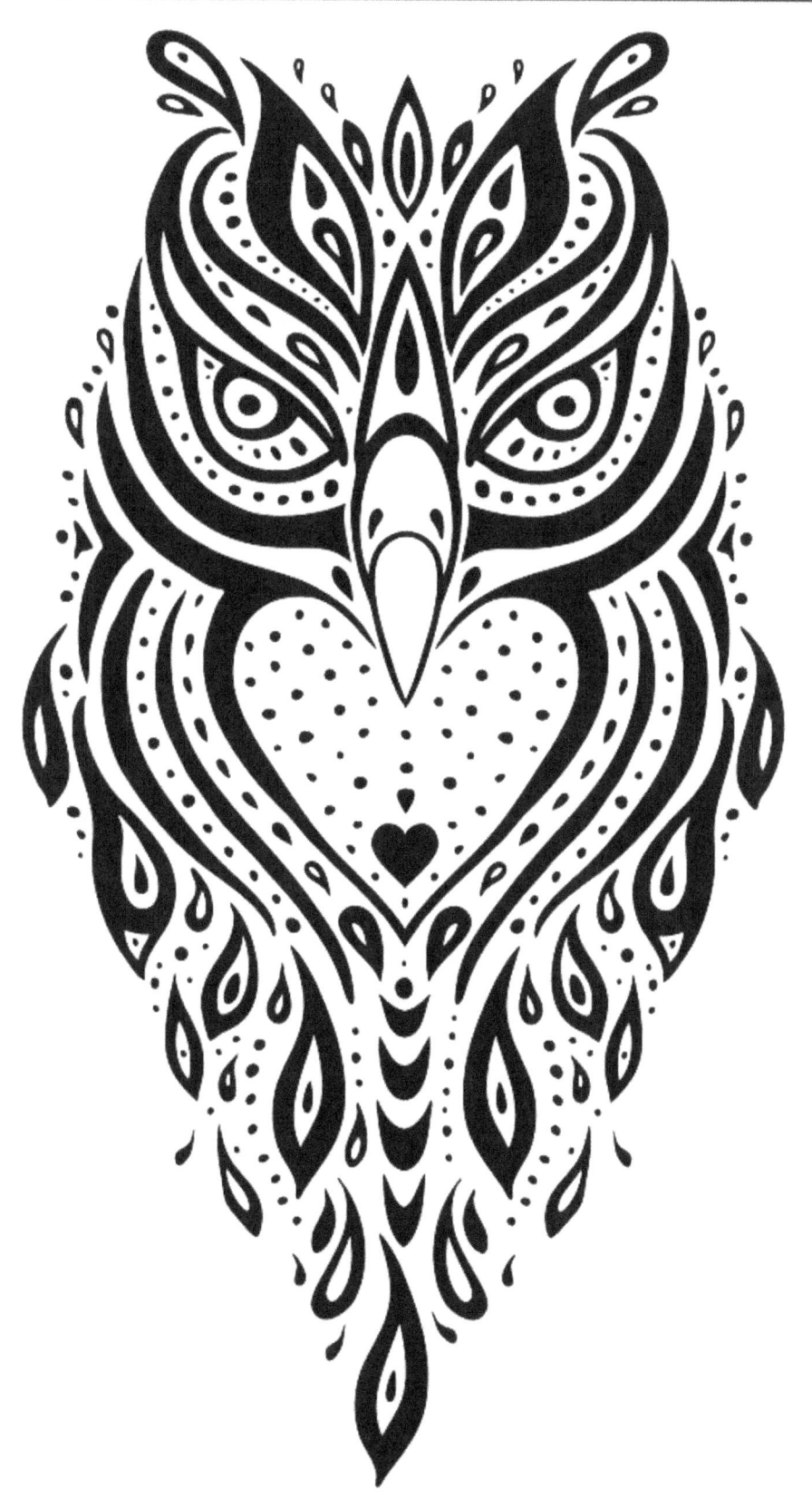

MIXED TATTOO COLORING BOOK

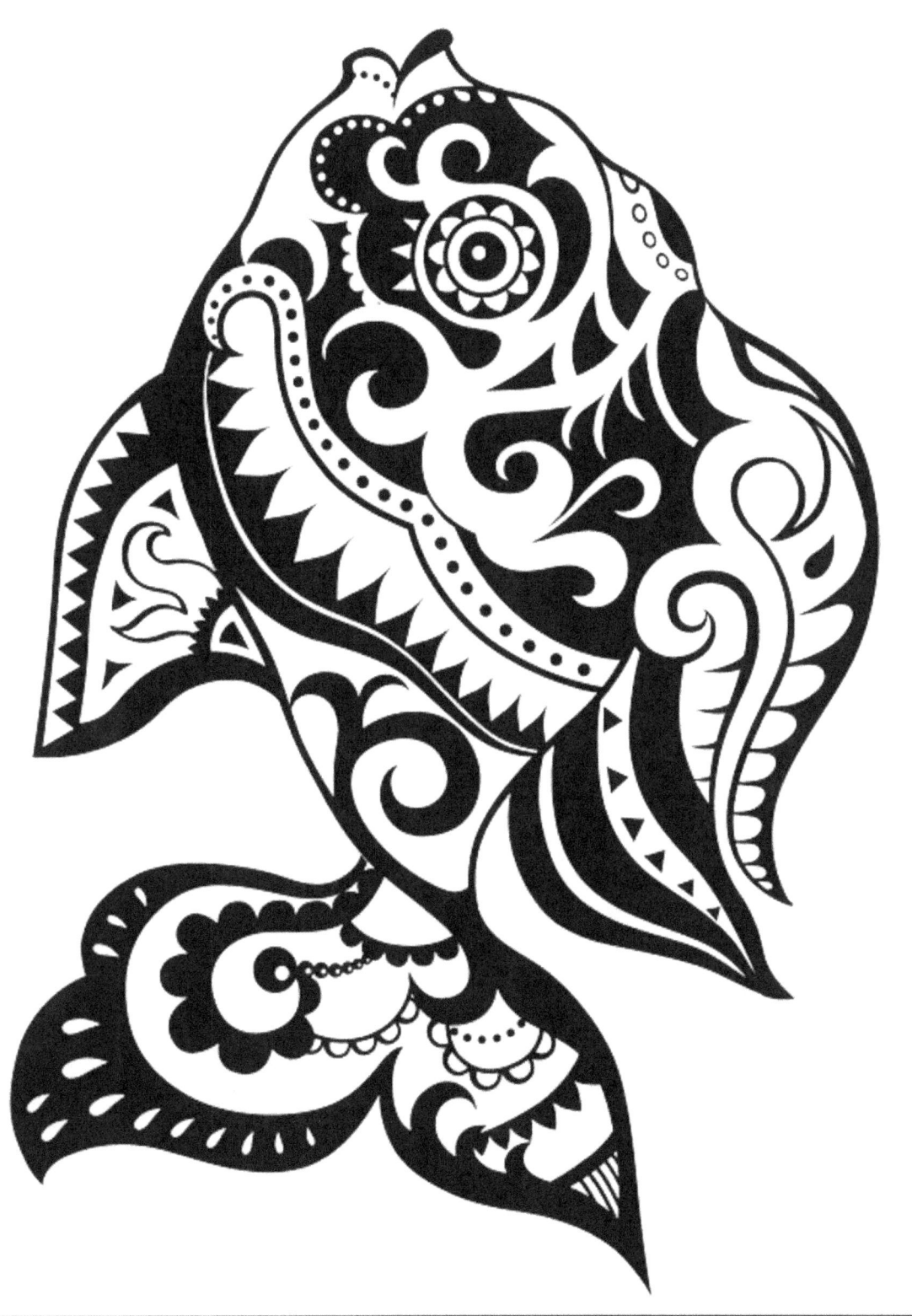

MIXED TATTOO COLORING BOOK

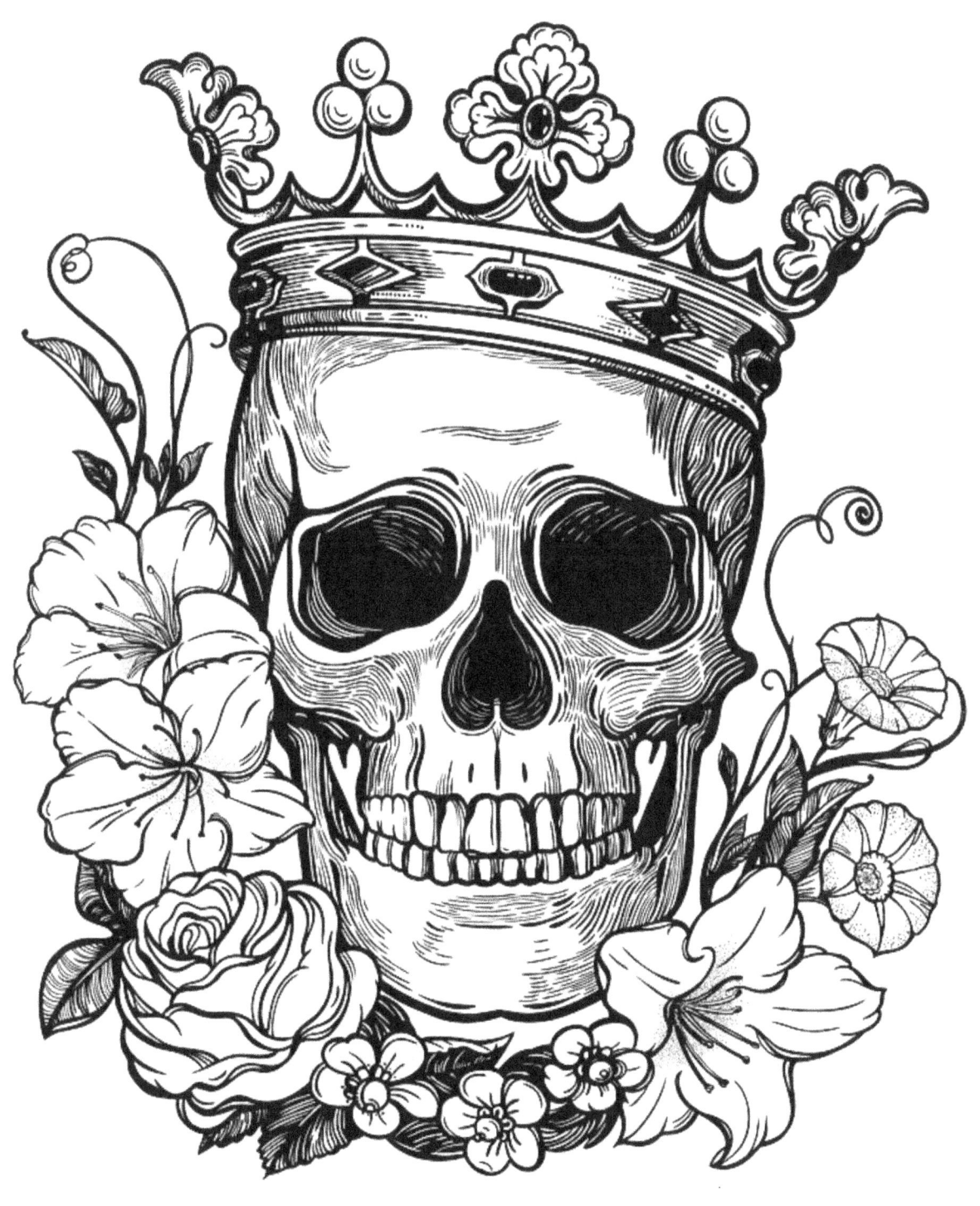

MIXED TATTOO COLORING BOOK

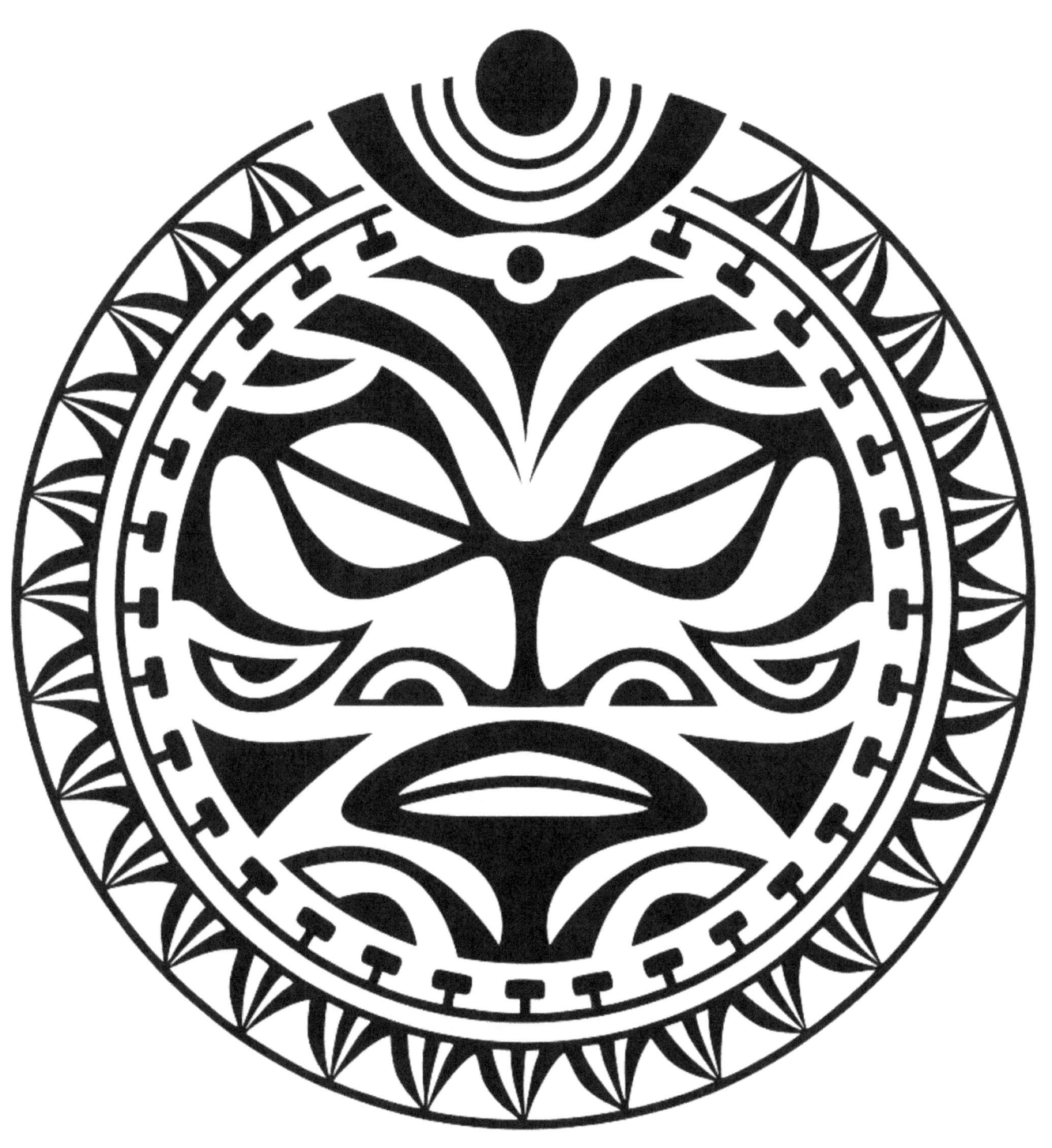

MIXED TATTOO COLORING BOOK

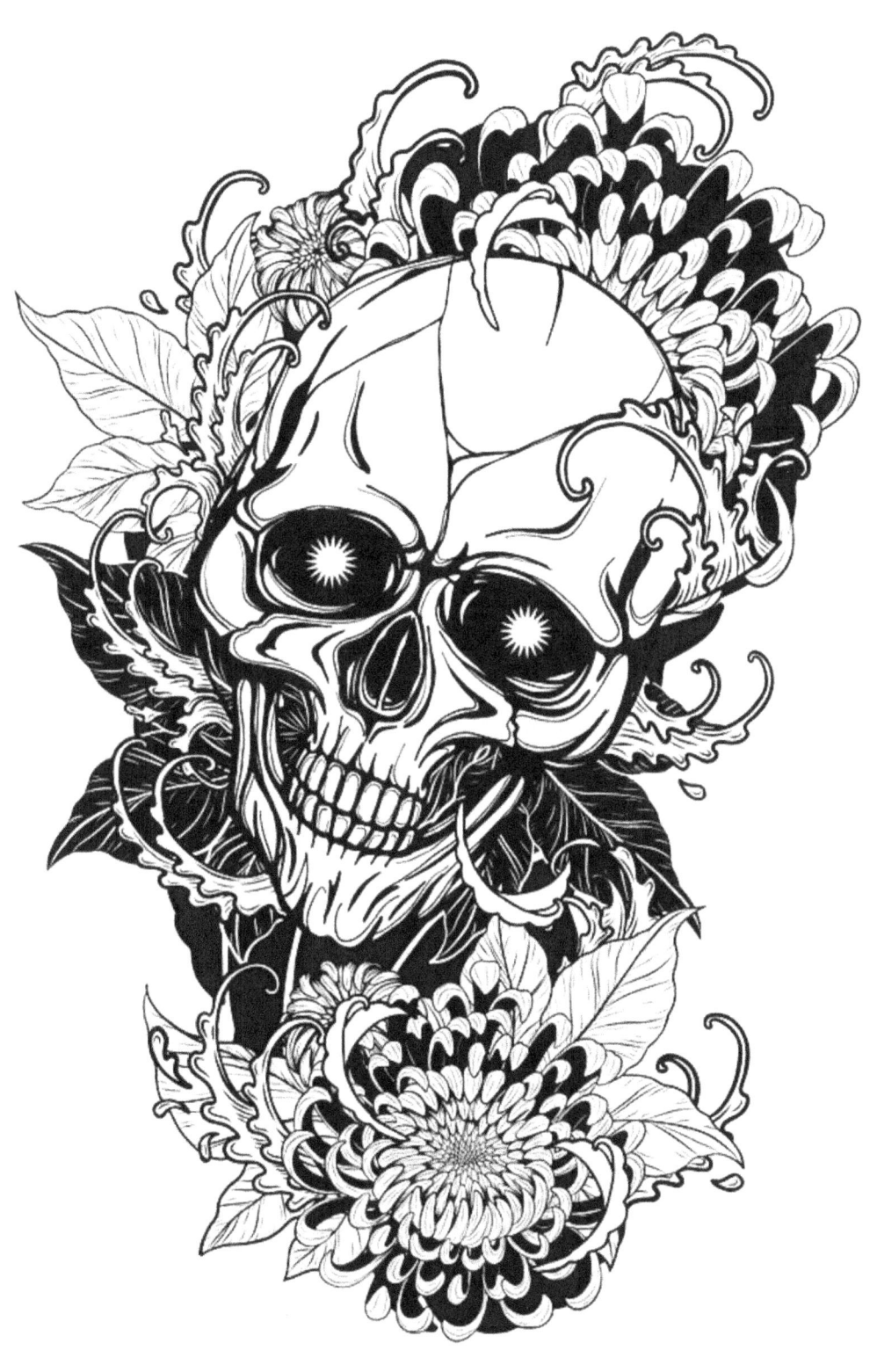

MIXED TATTOO COLORING BOOK

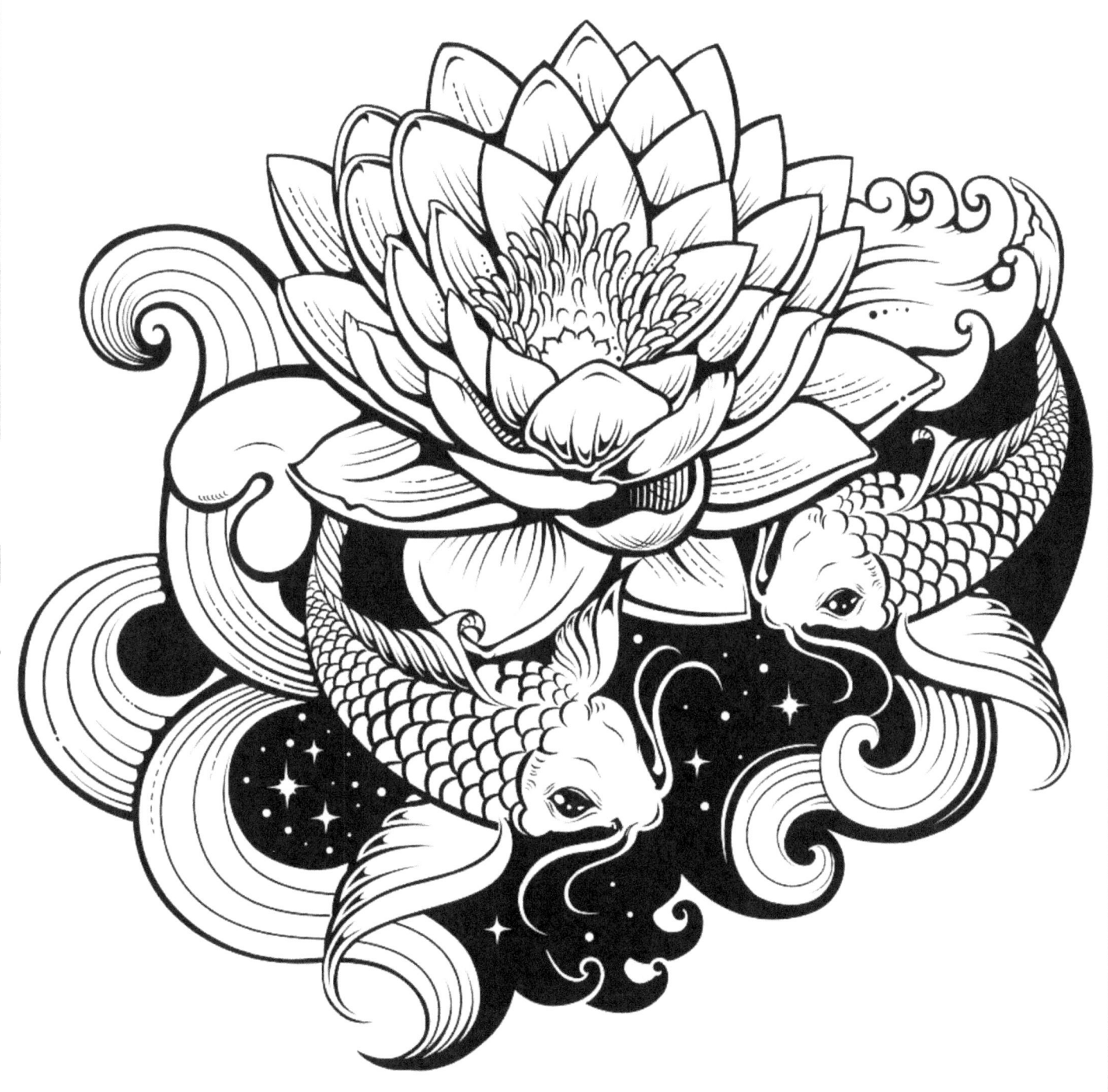

MIXED TATTOO COLORING BOOK

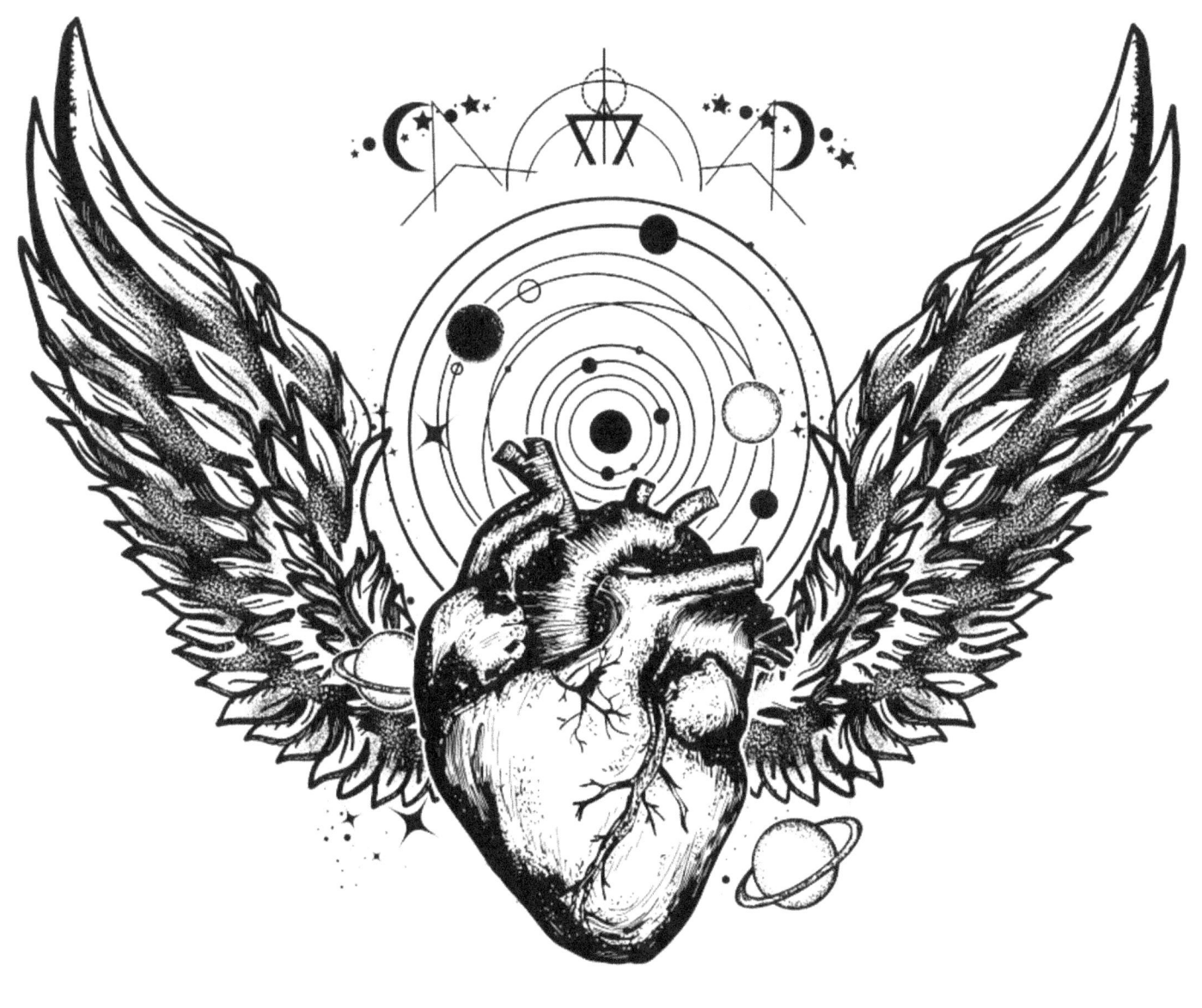

MIXED TATTOO COLORING BOOK

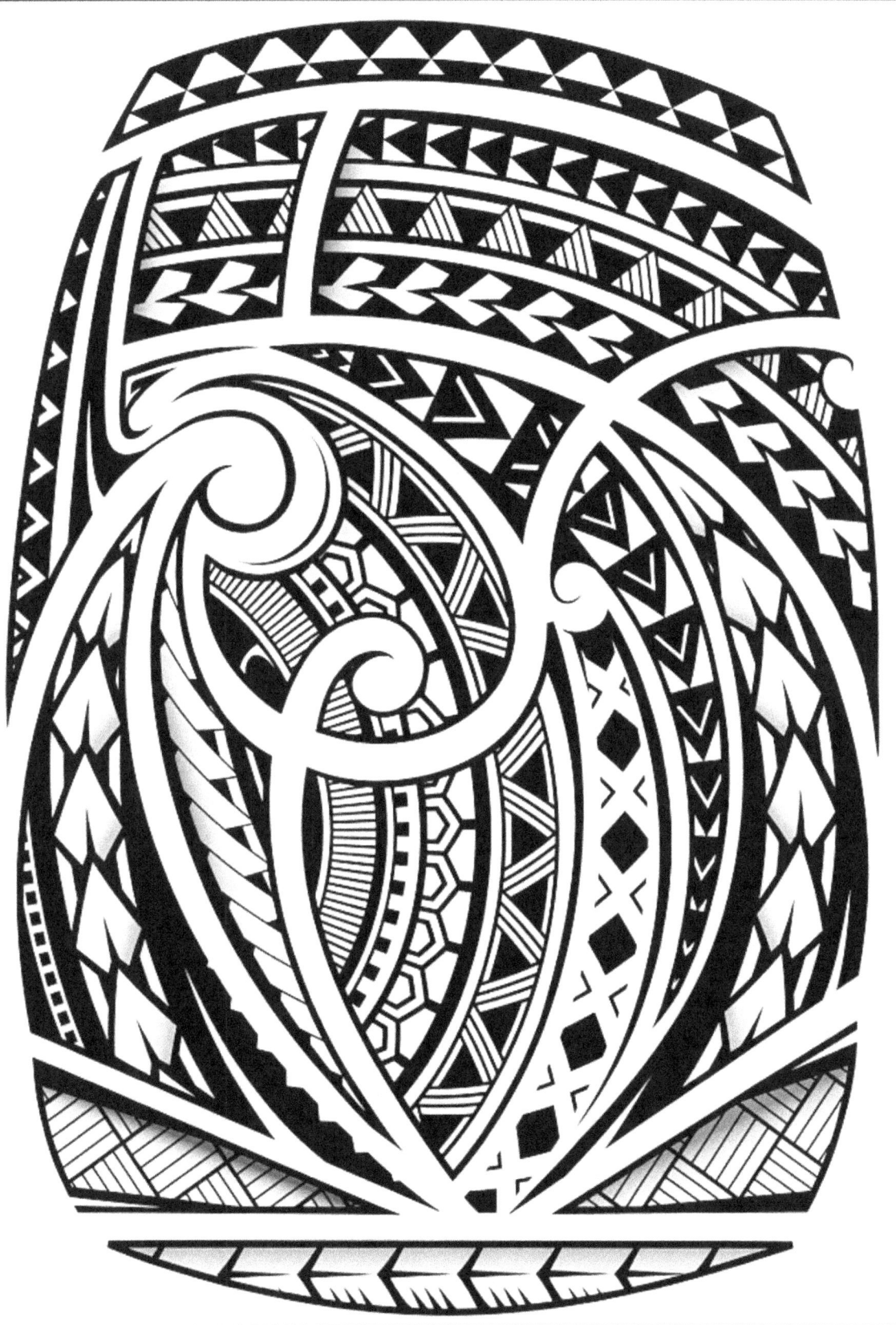

MIXED TATTOO COLORING BOOK

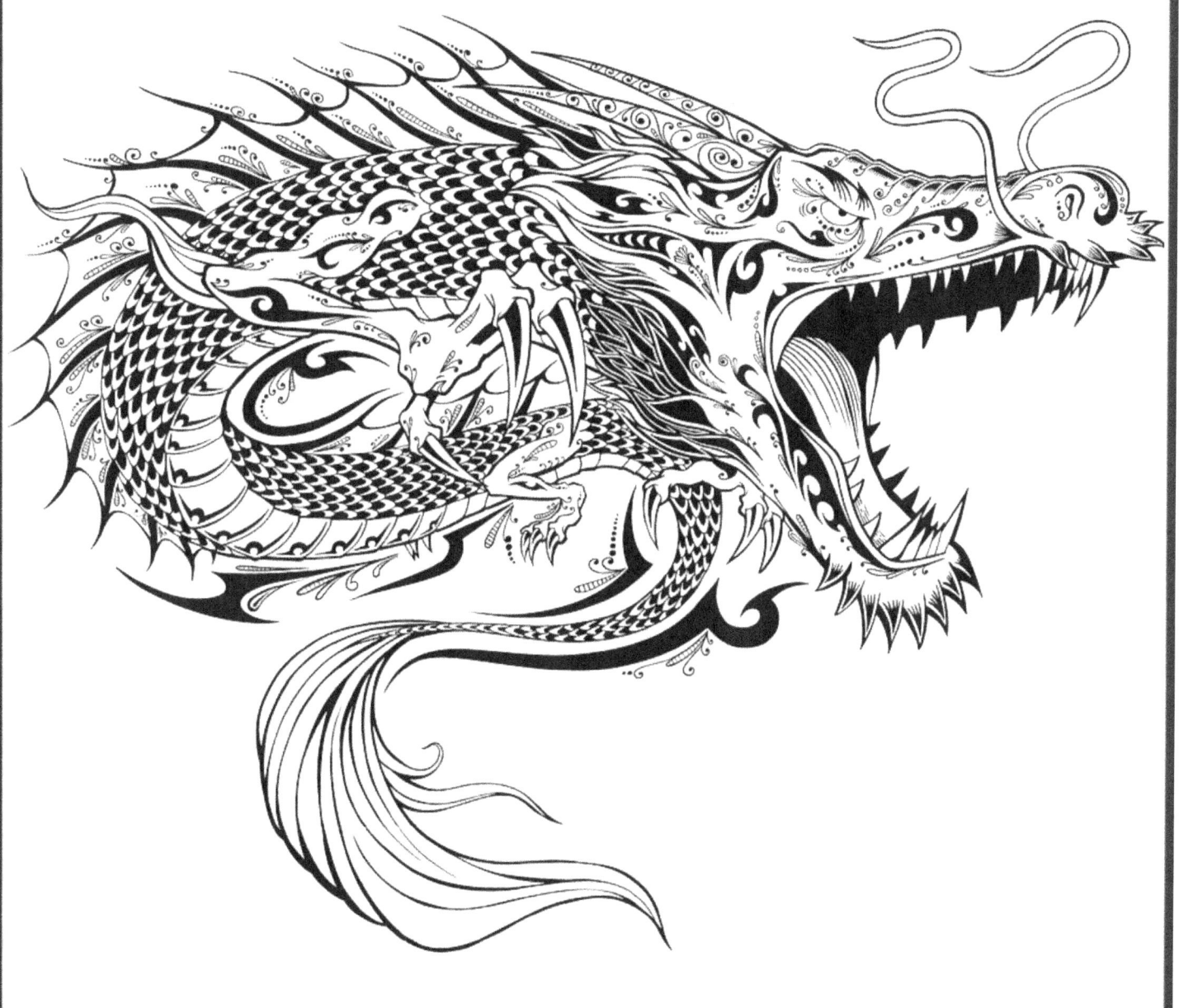

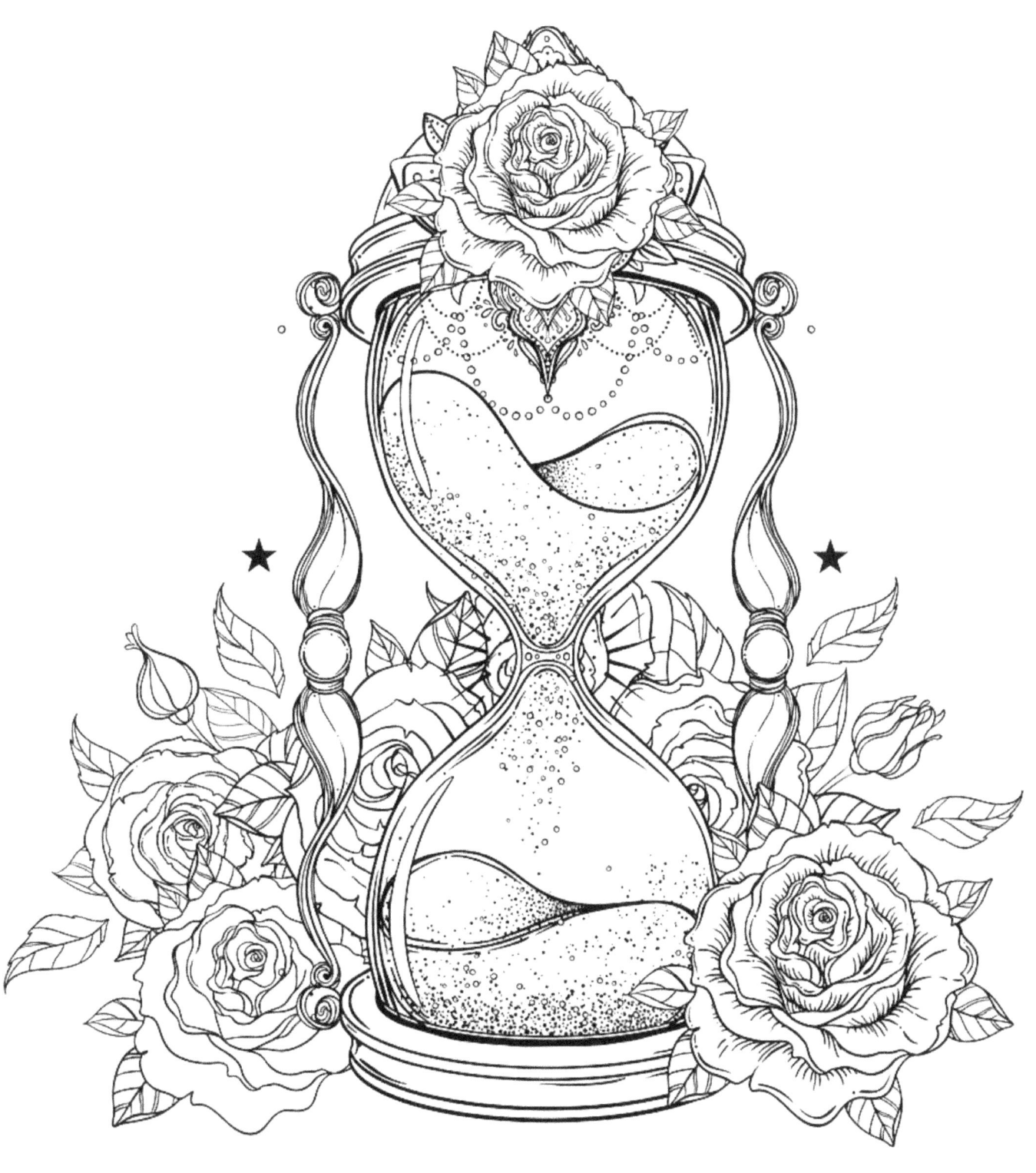

MIXED TATTOO COLORING BOOK

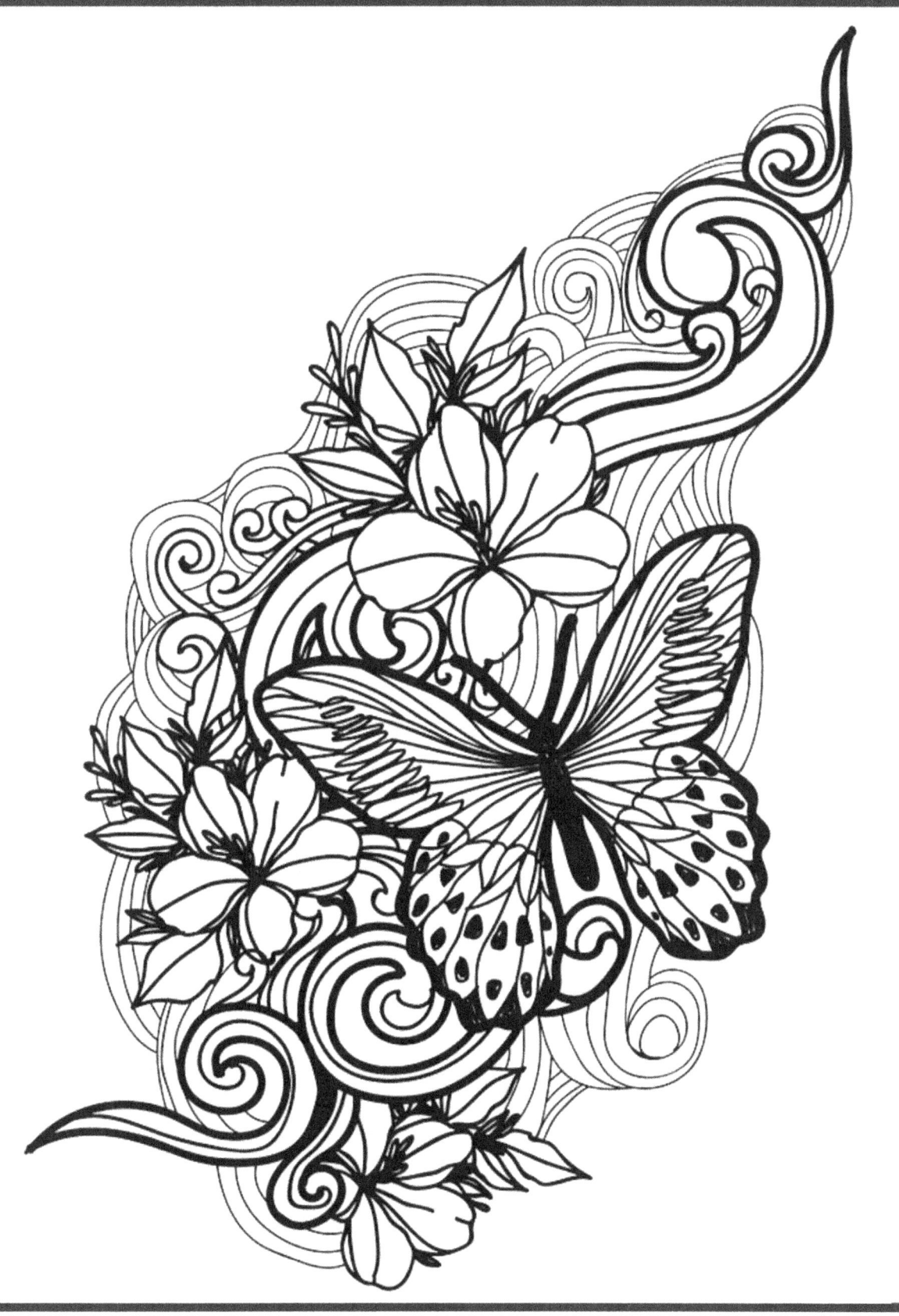

MIXED TATTOO COLORING BOOK

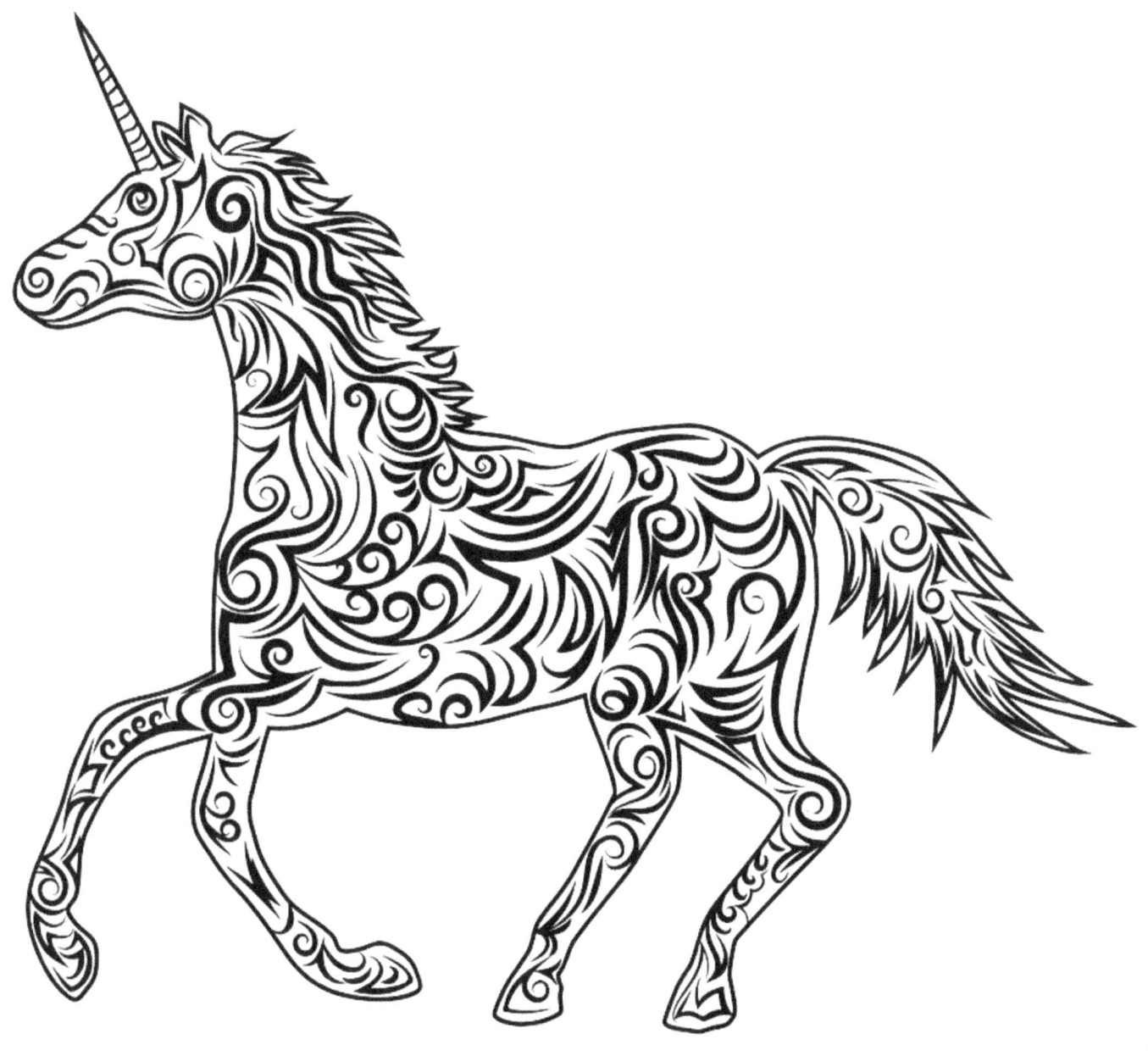

MIXED TATTOO COLORING BOOK

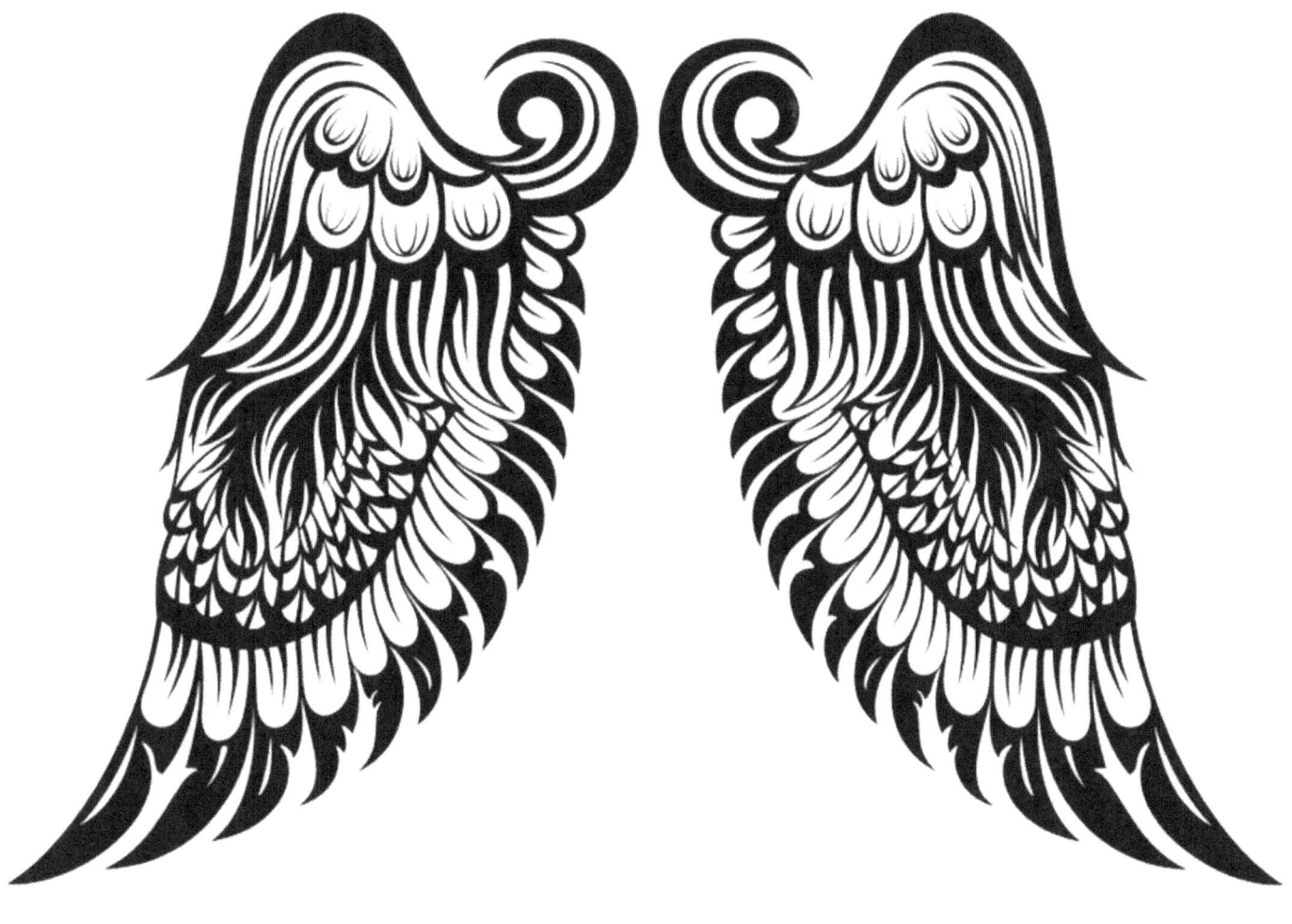

MIXED TATTOO COLORING BOOK

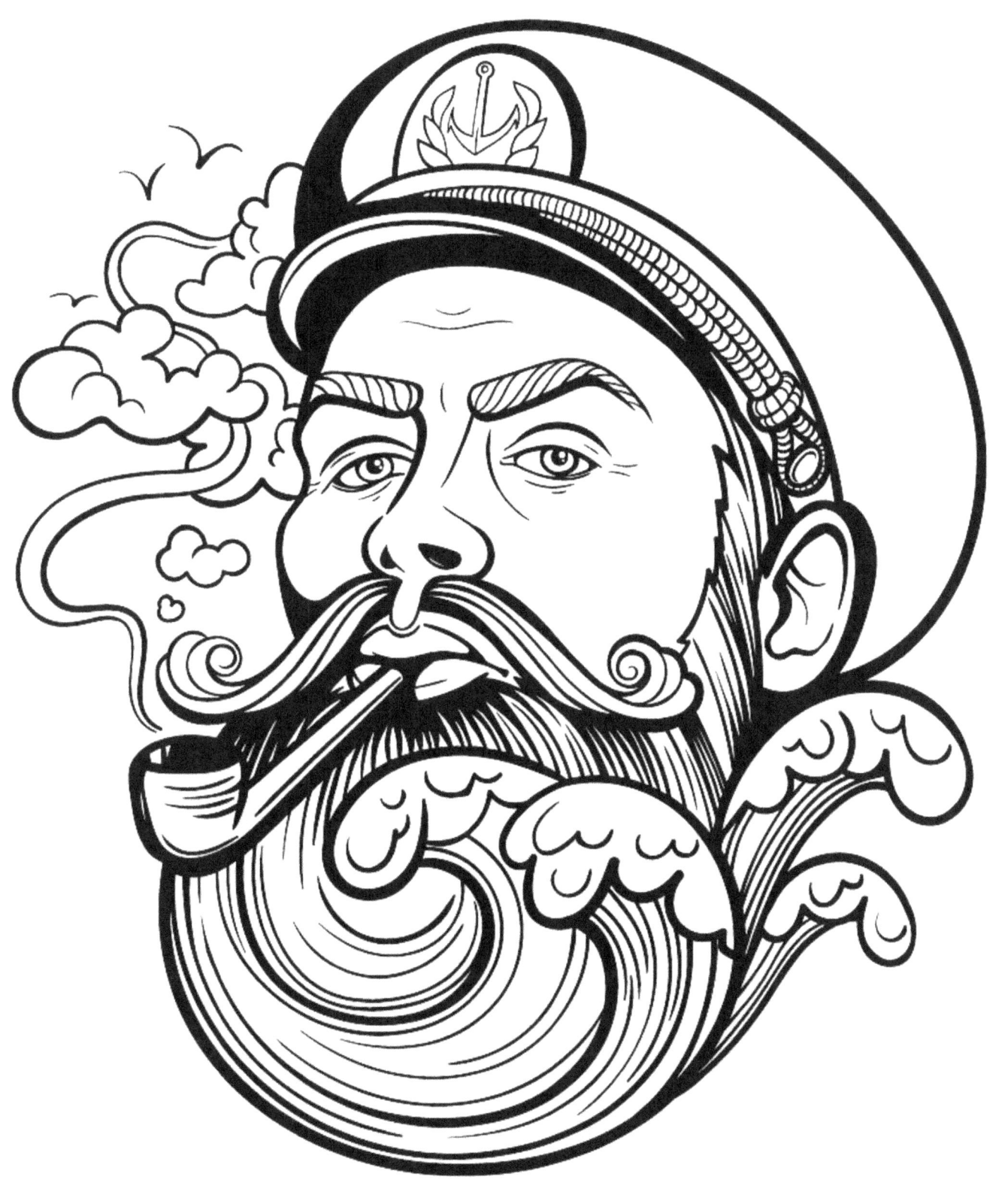

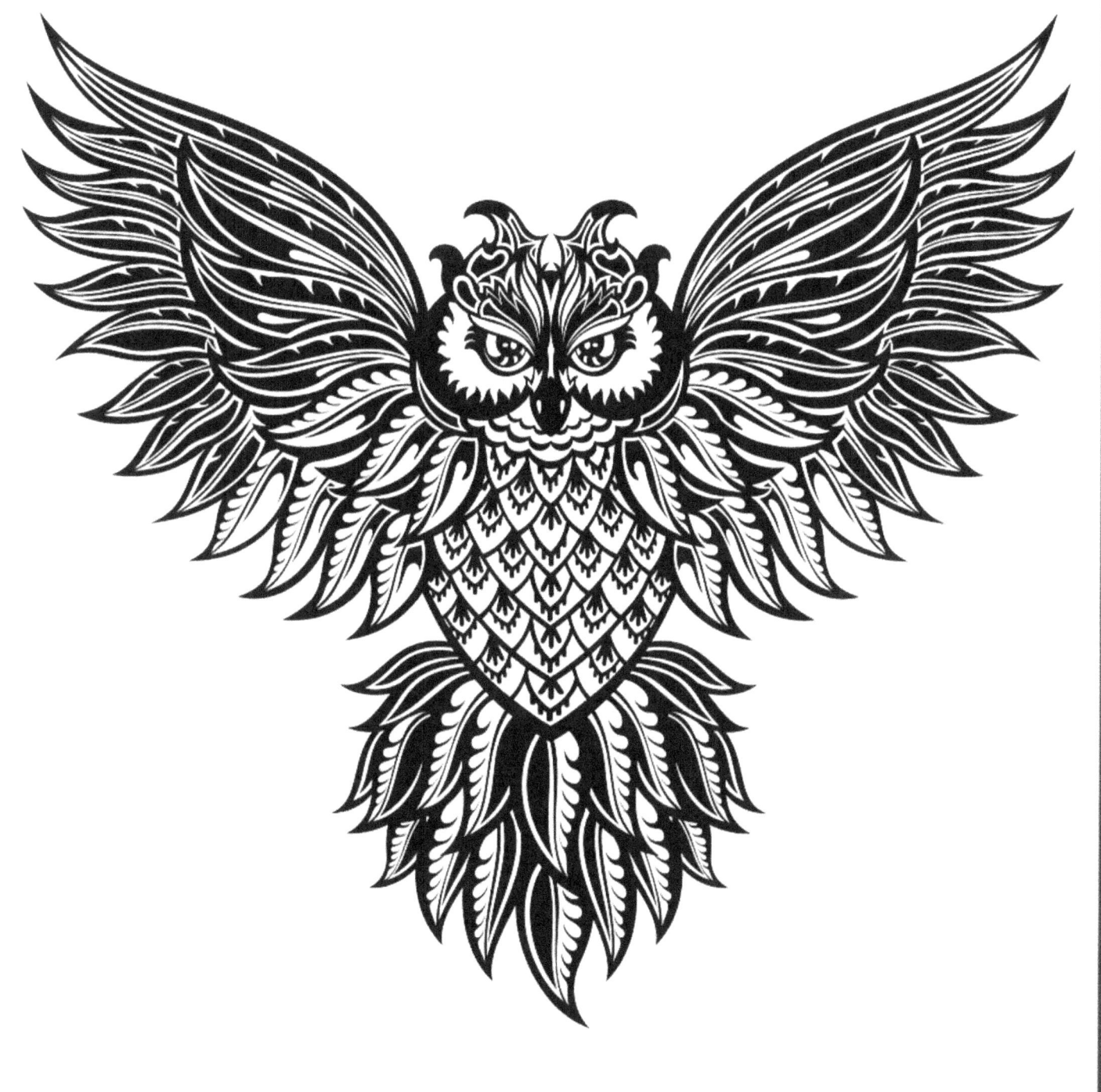

MIXED TATTOO COLORING BOOK

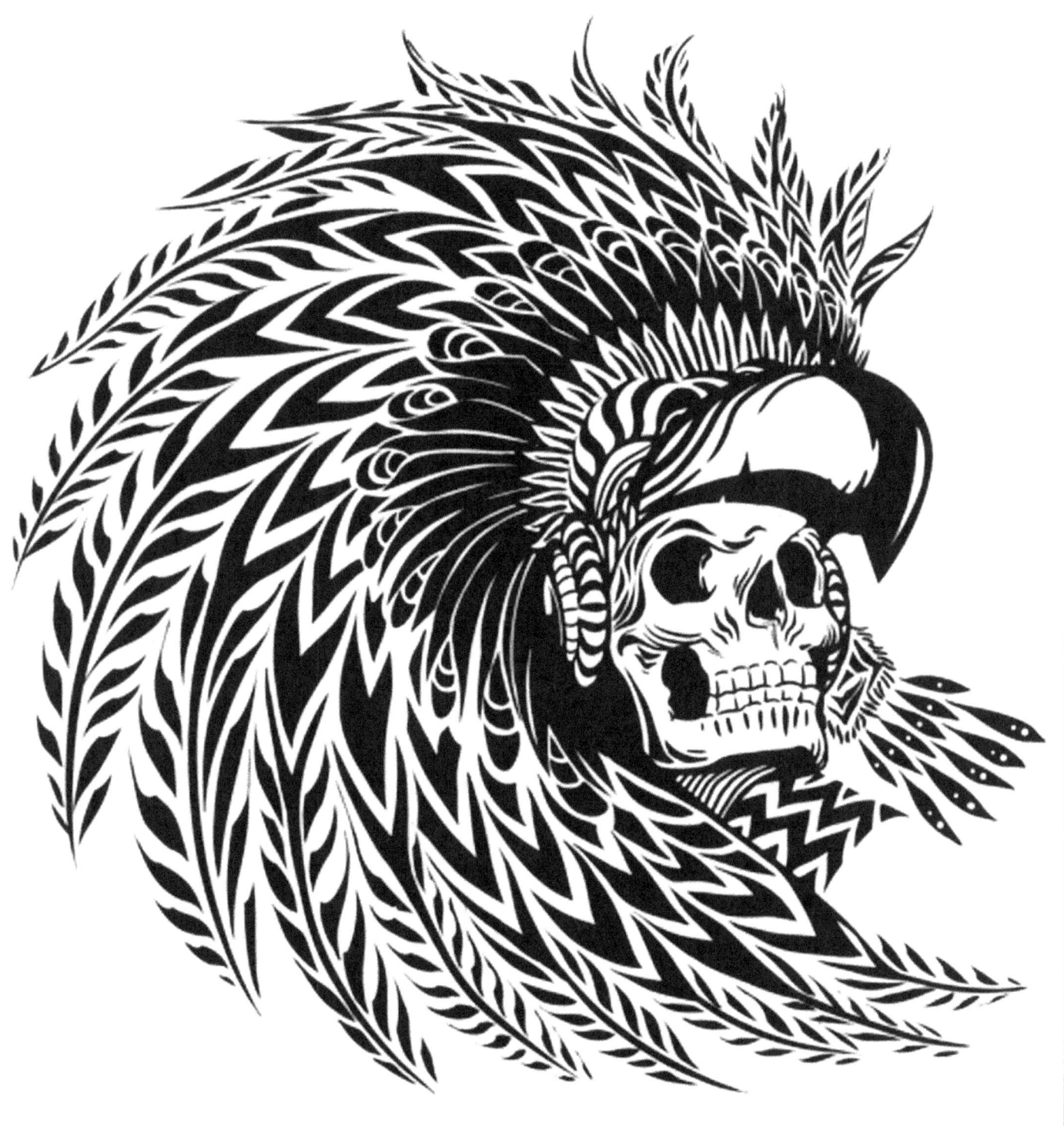

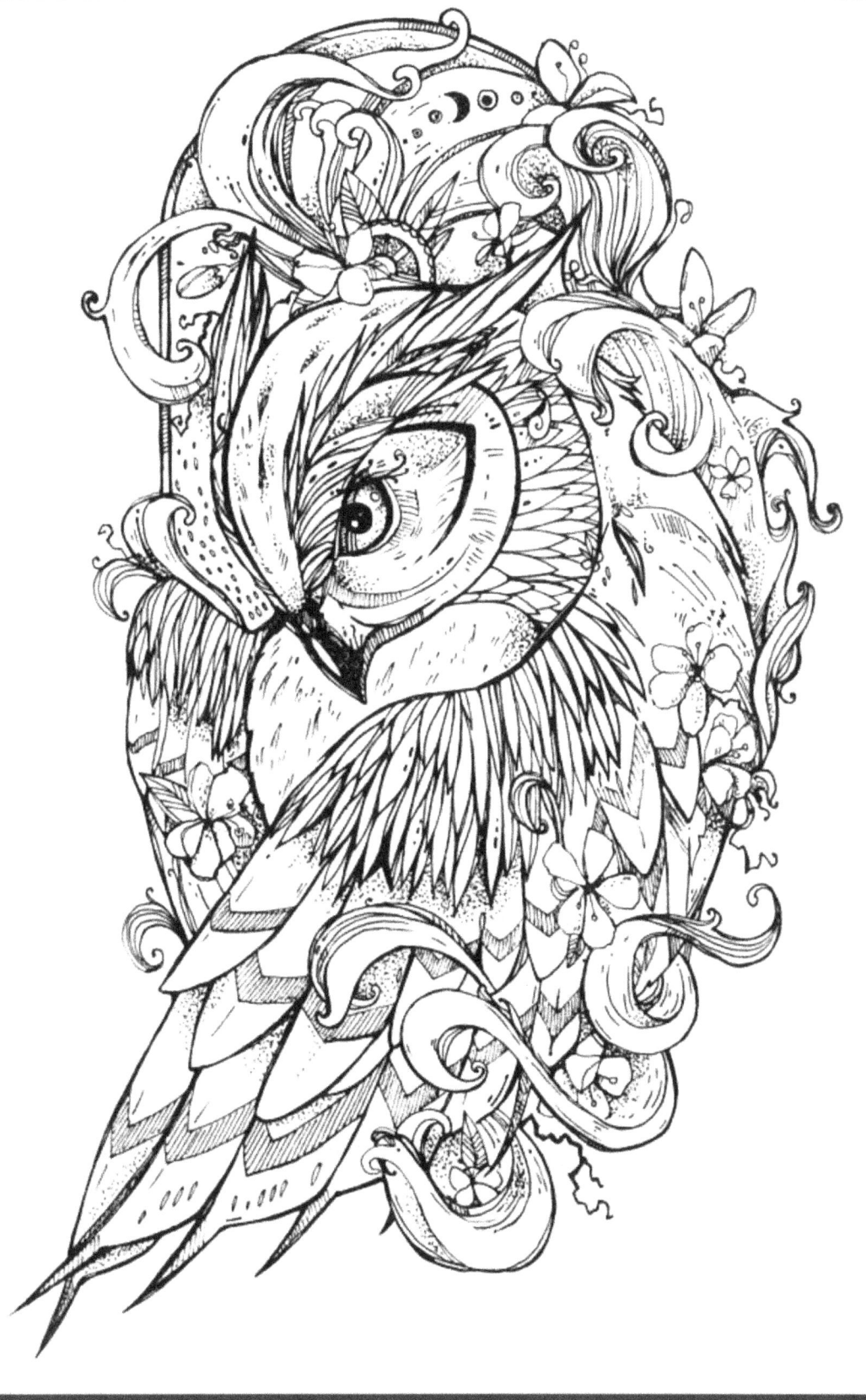

MIXED TATTOO COLORING BOOK

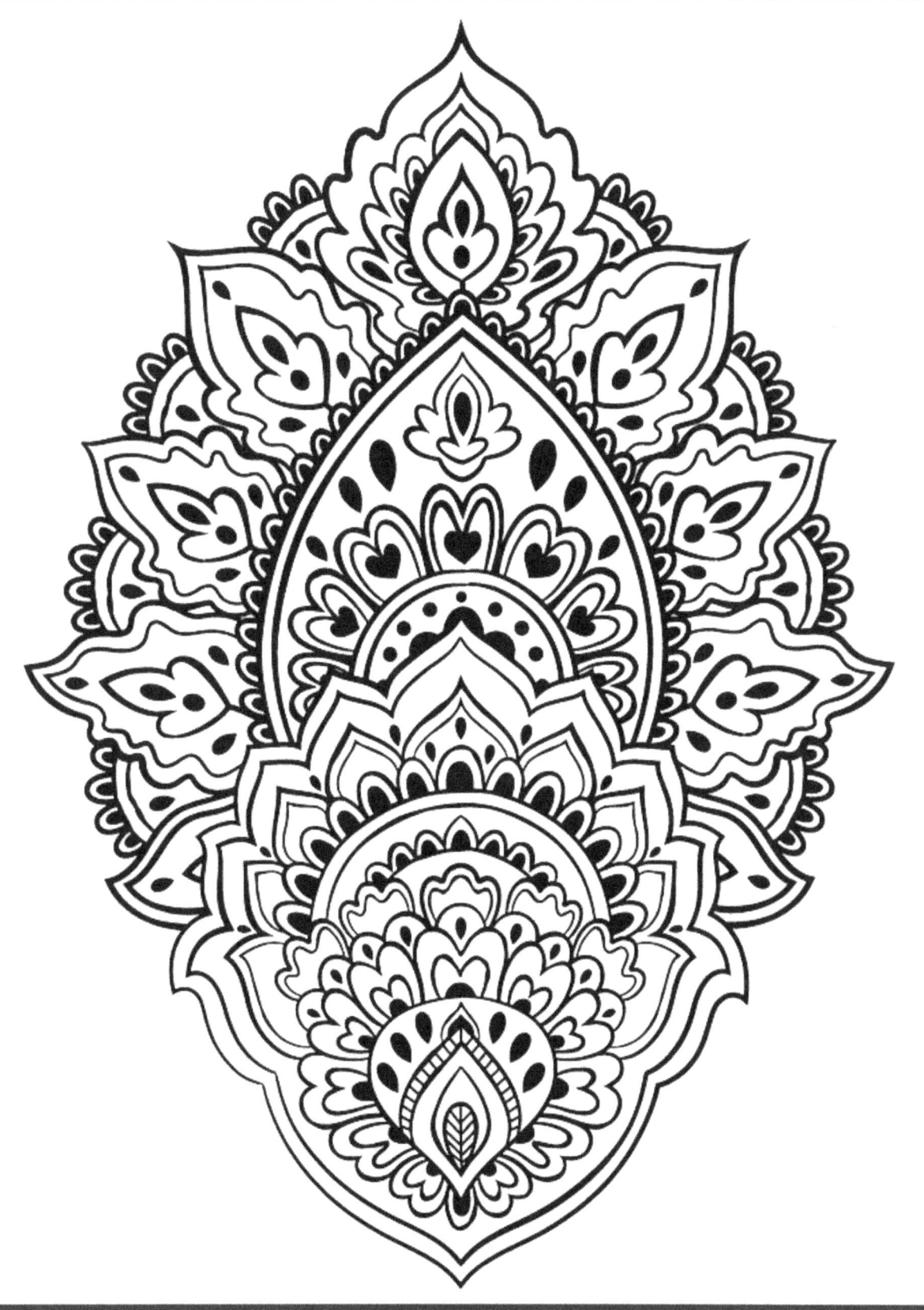

MIXED TATTOO COLORING BOOK

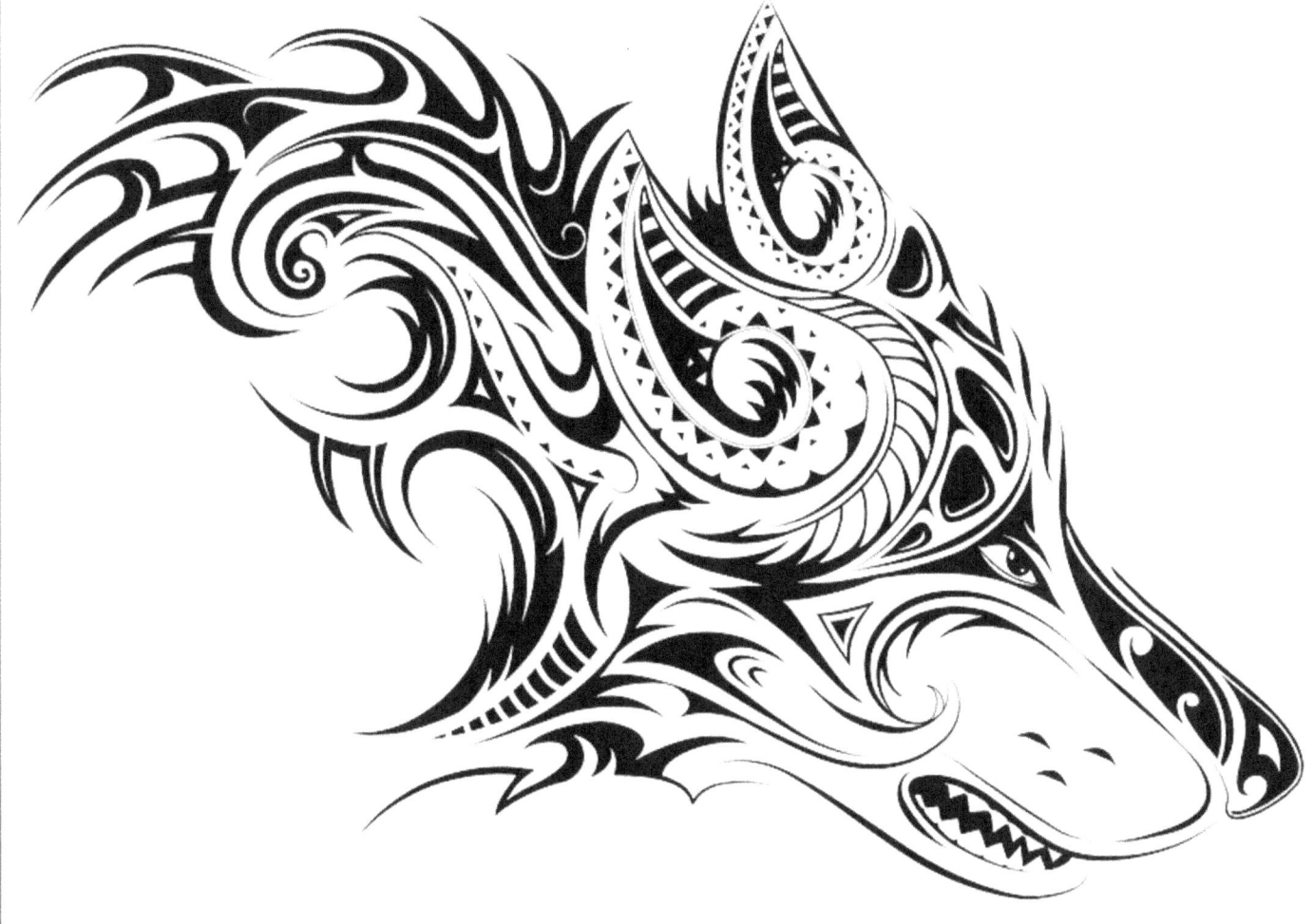

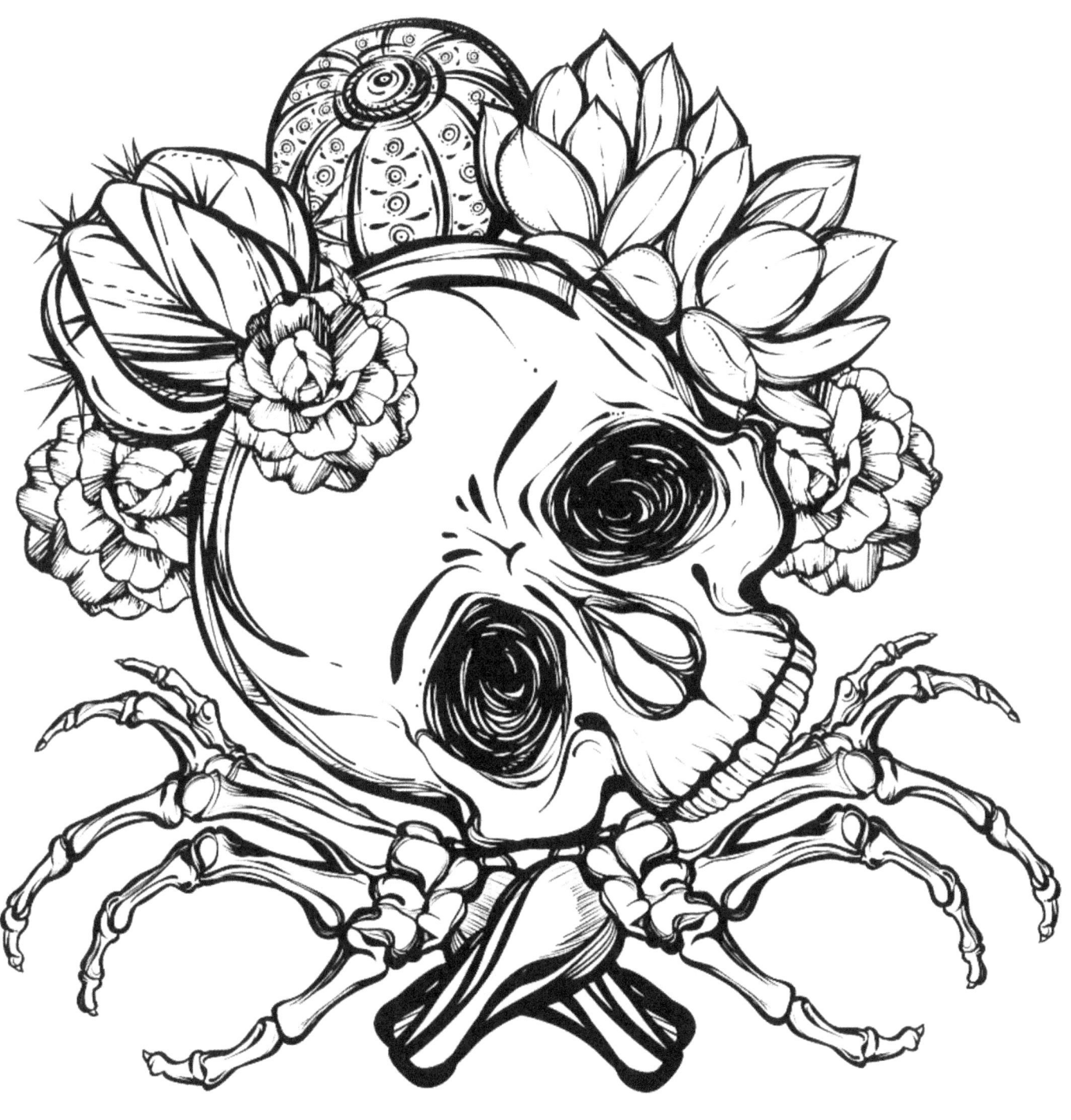

MIXED TATTOO COLORING BOOK

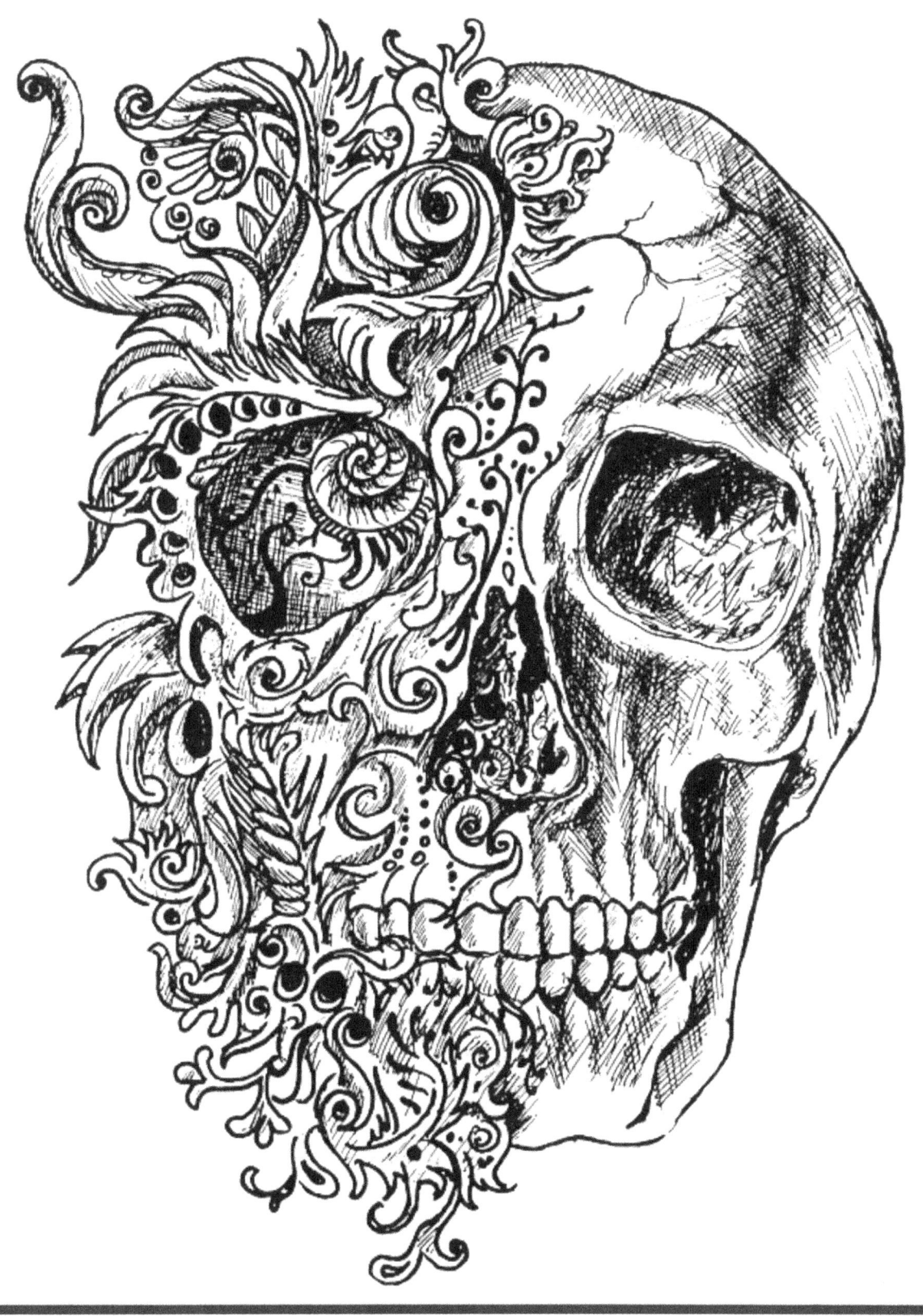

MIXED TATTOO COLORING BOOK

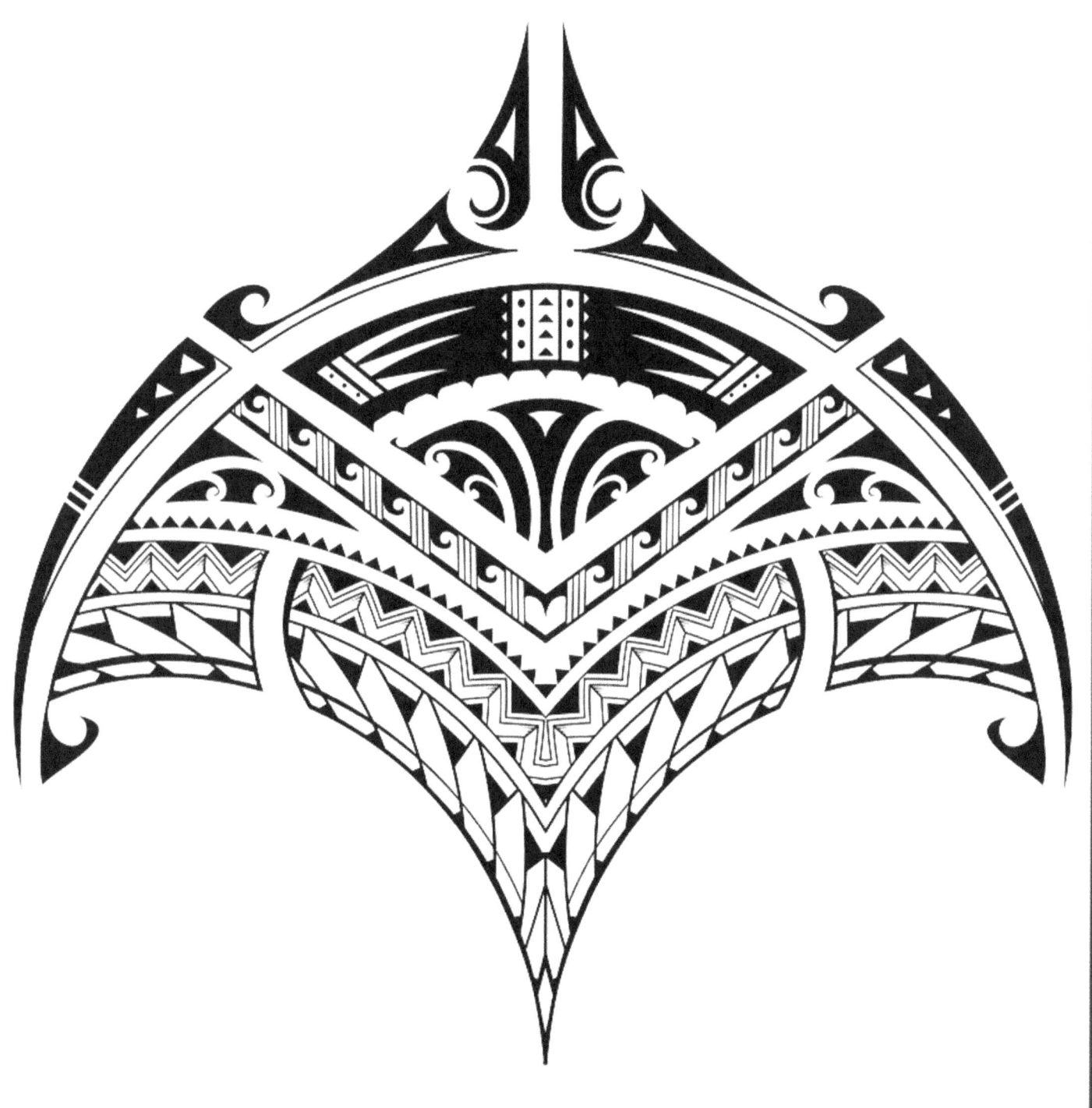

MIXED TATTOO COLORING BOOK

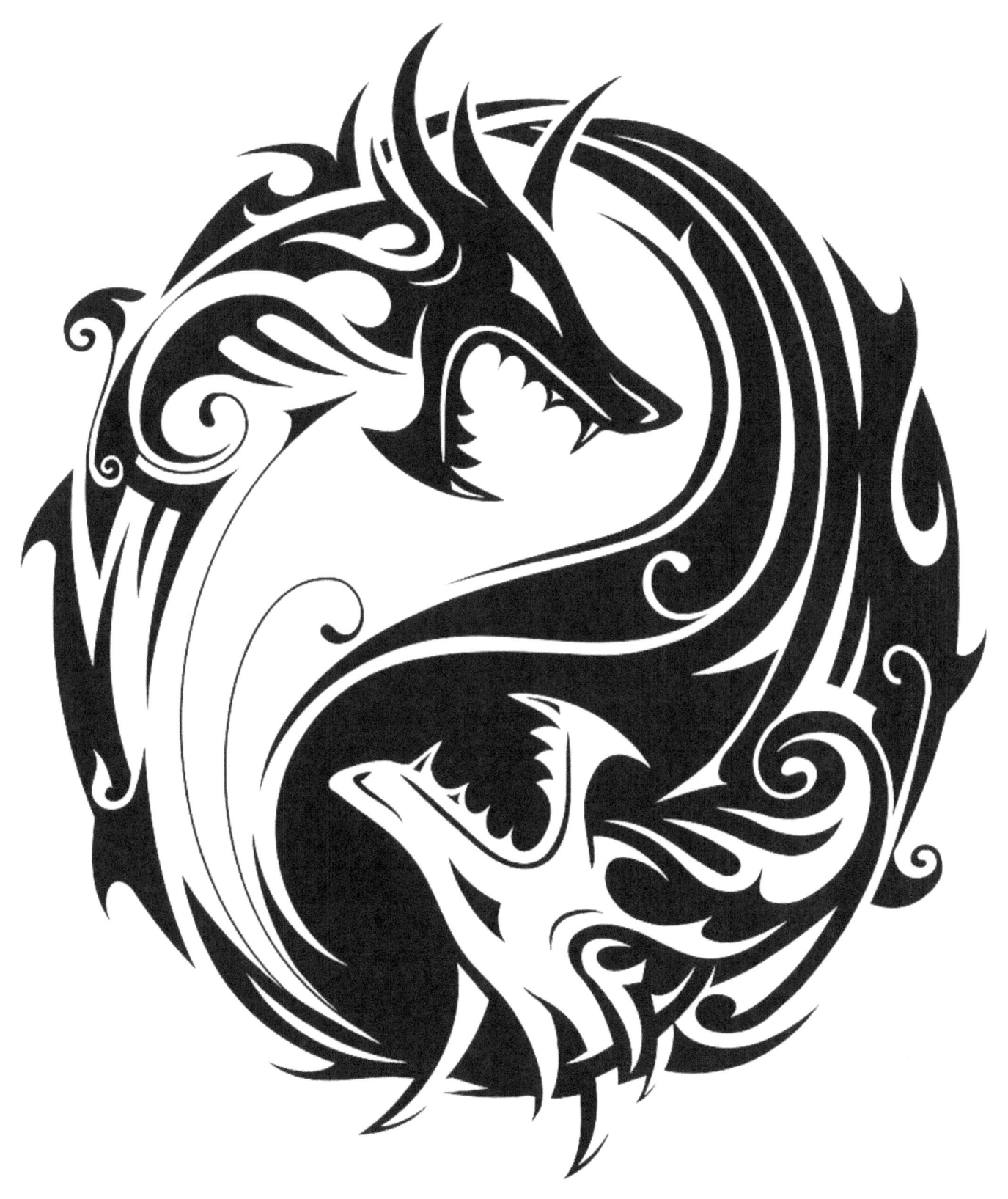

MIXED TATTOO COLORING BOOK

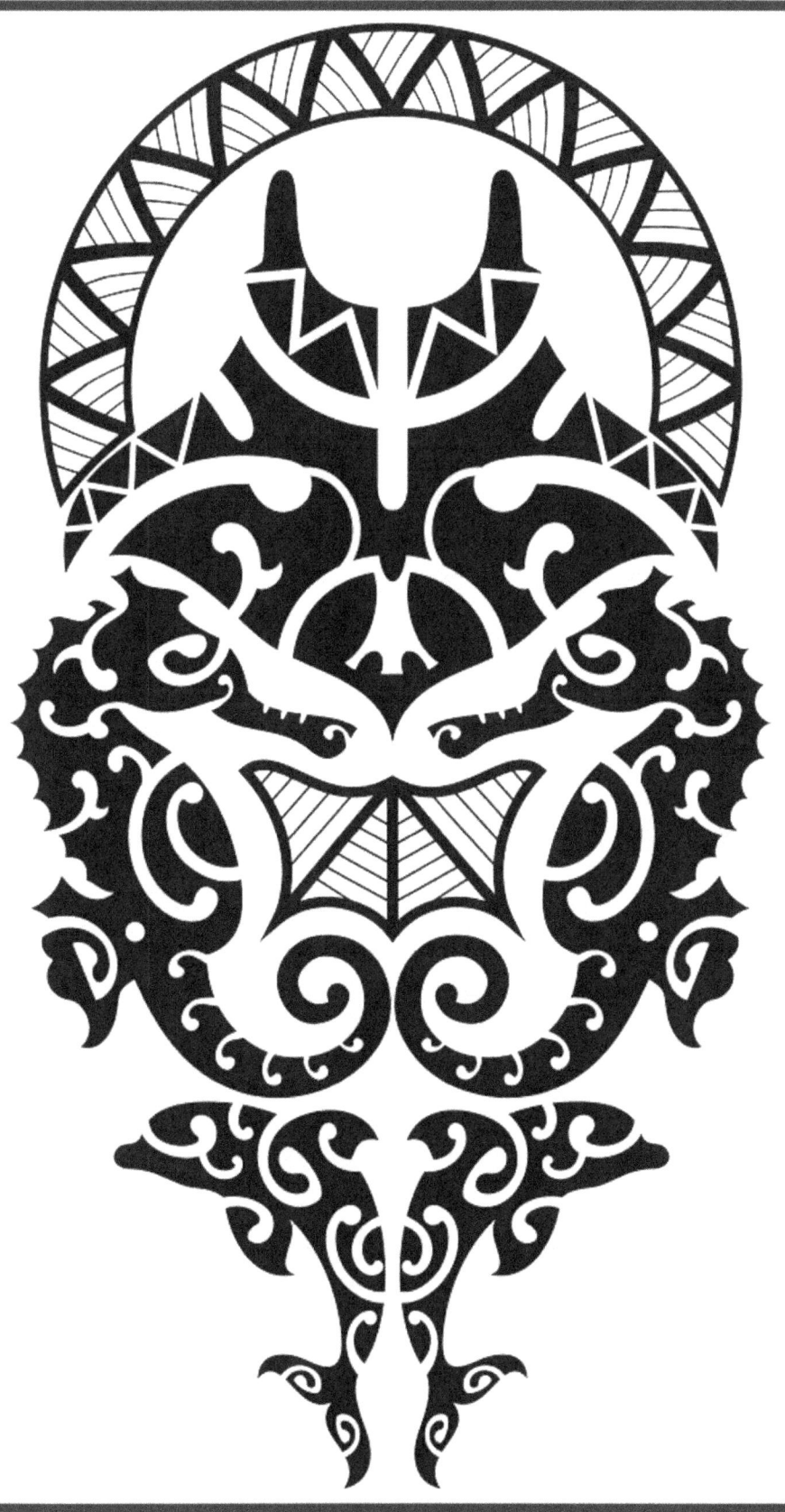

MIXED TATTOO COLORING BOOK

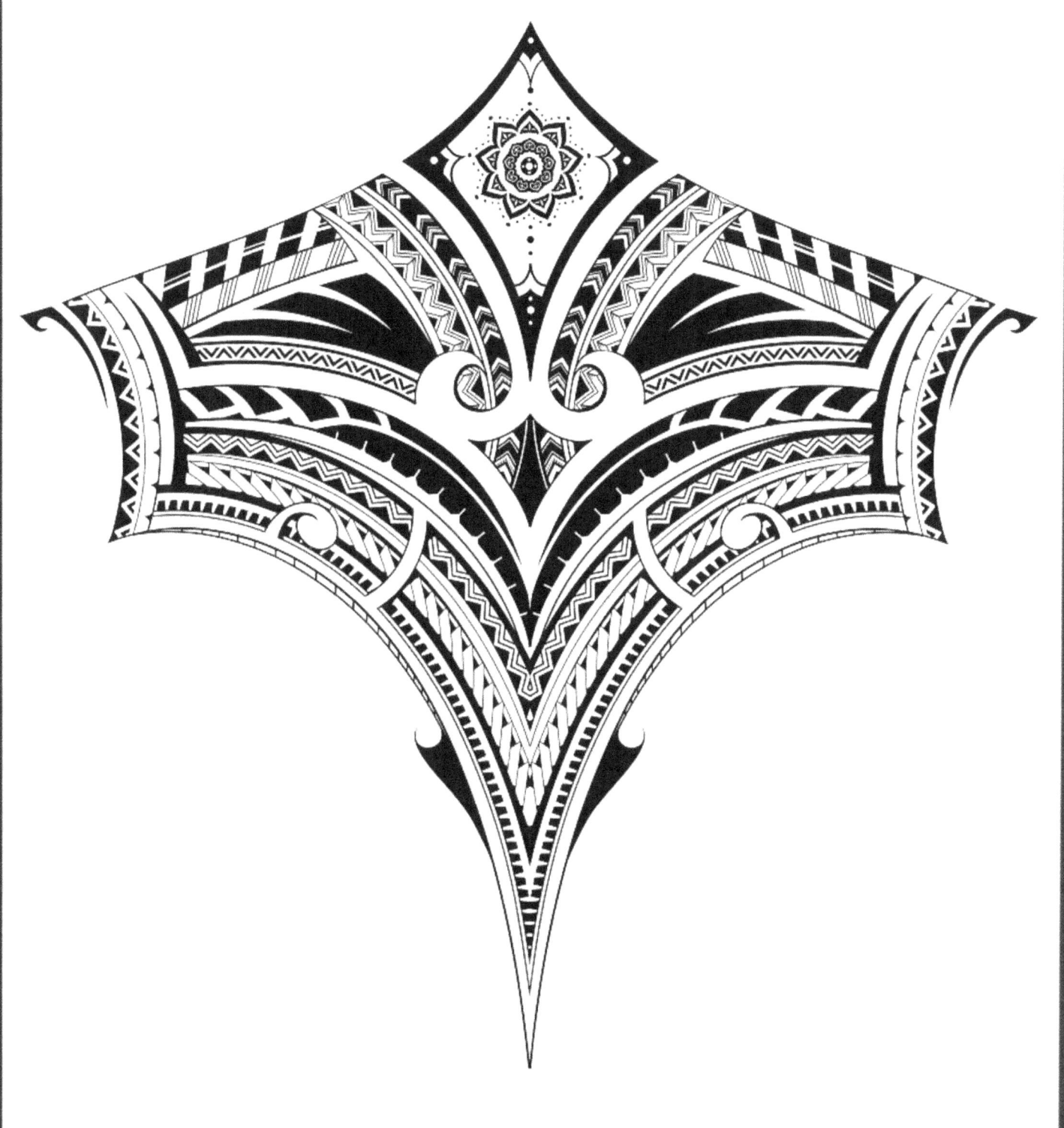

MIXED TATTOO COLORING BOOK

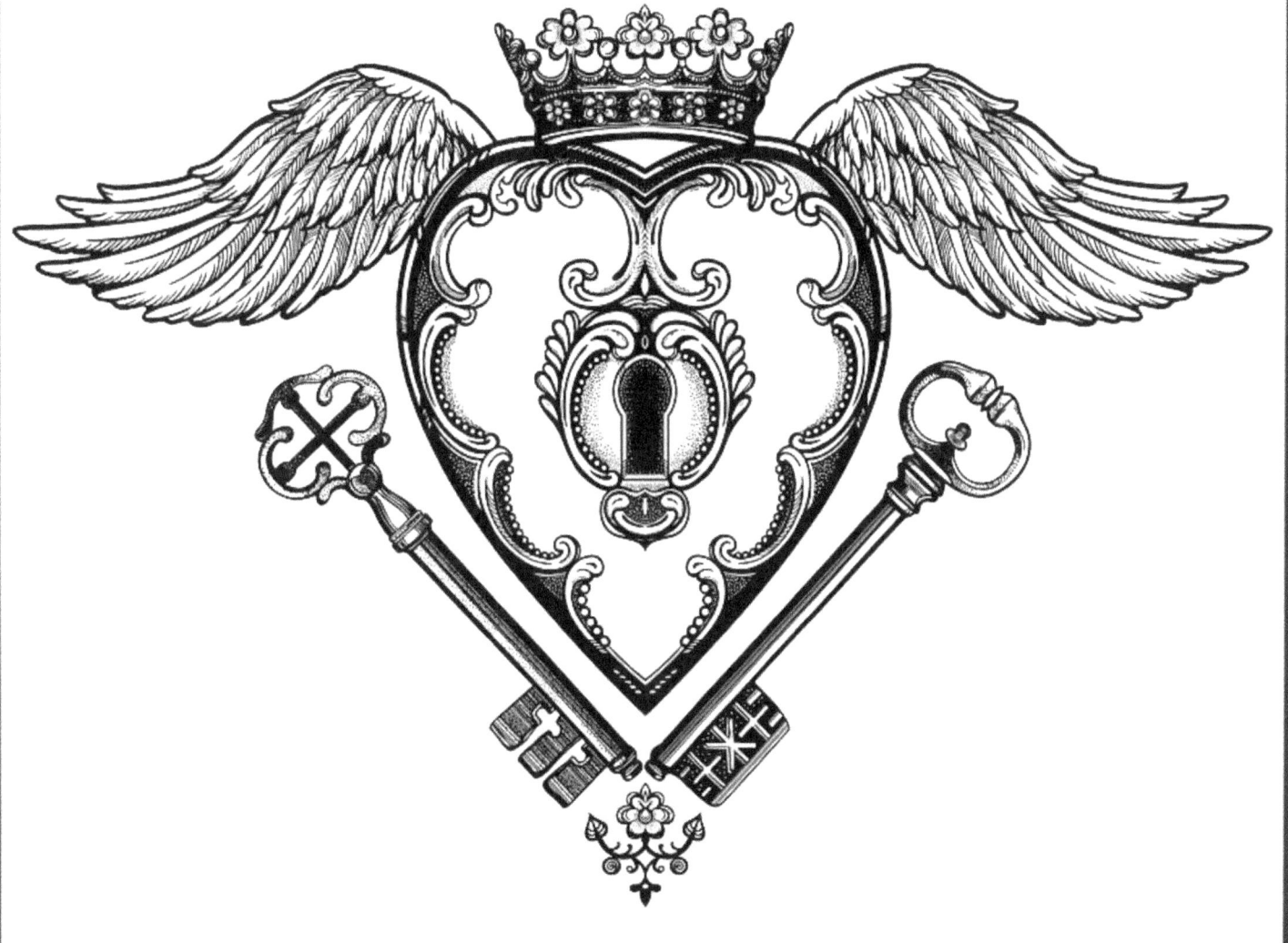

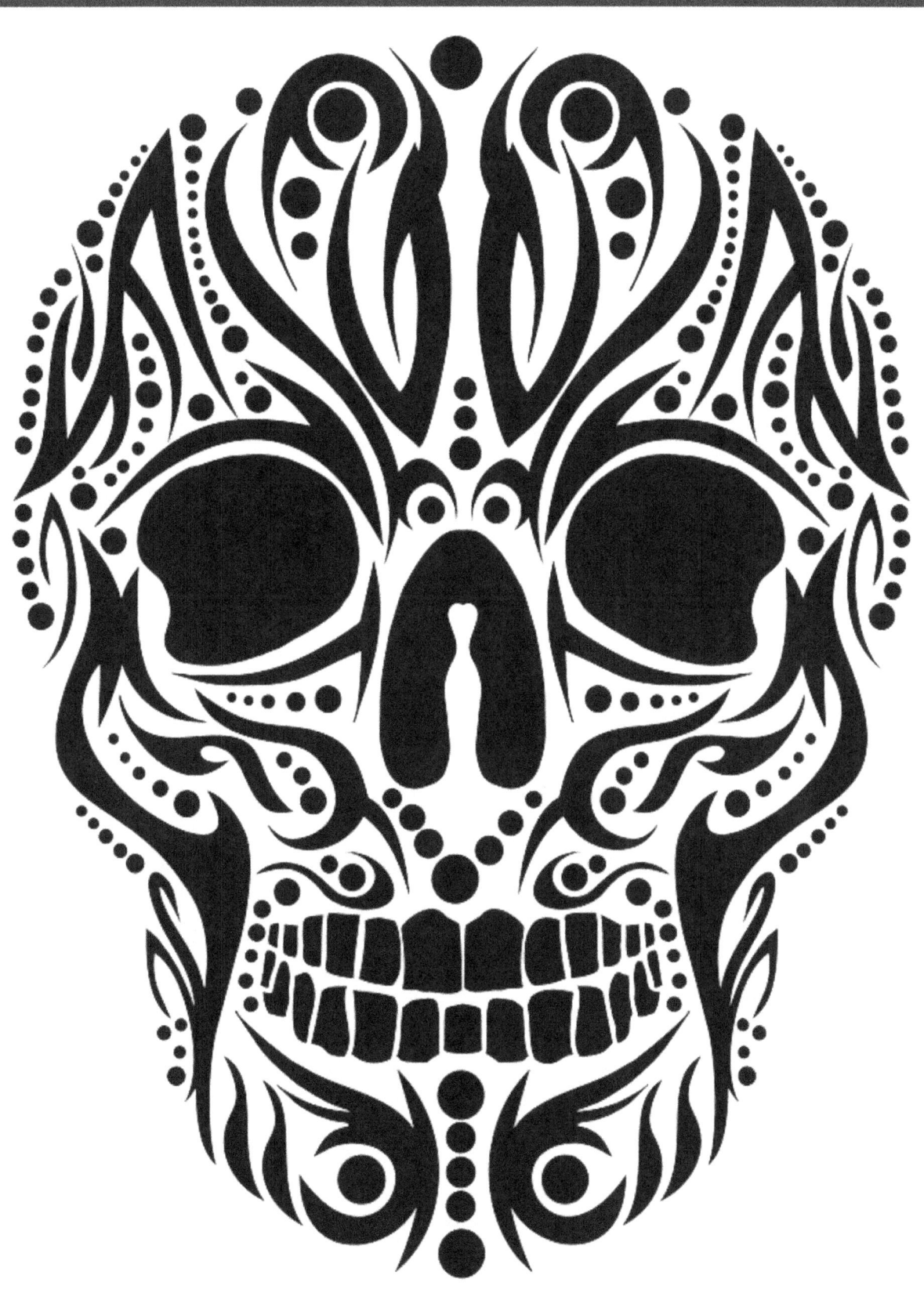

MIXED TATTOO COLORING BOOK

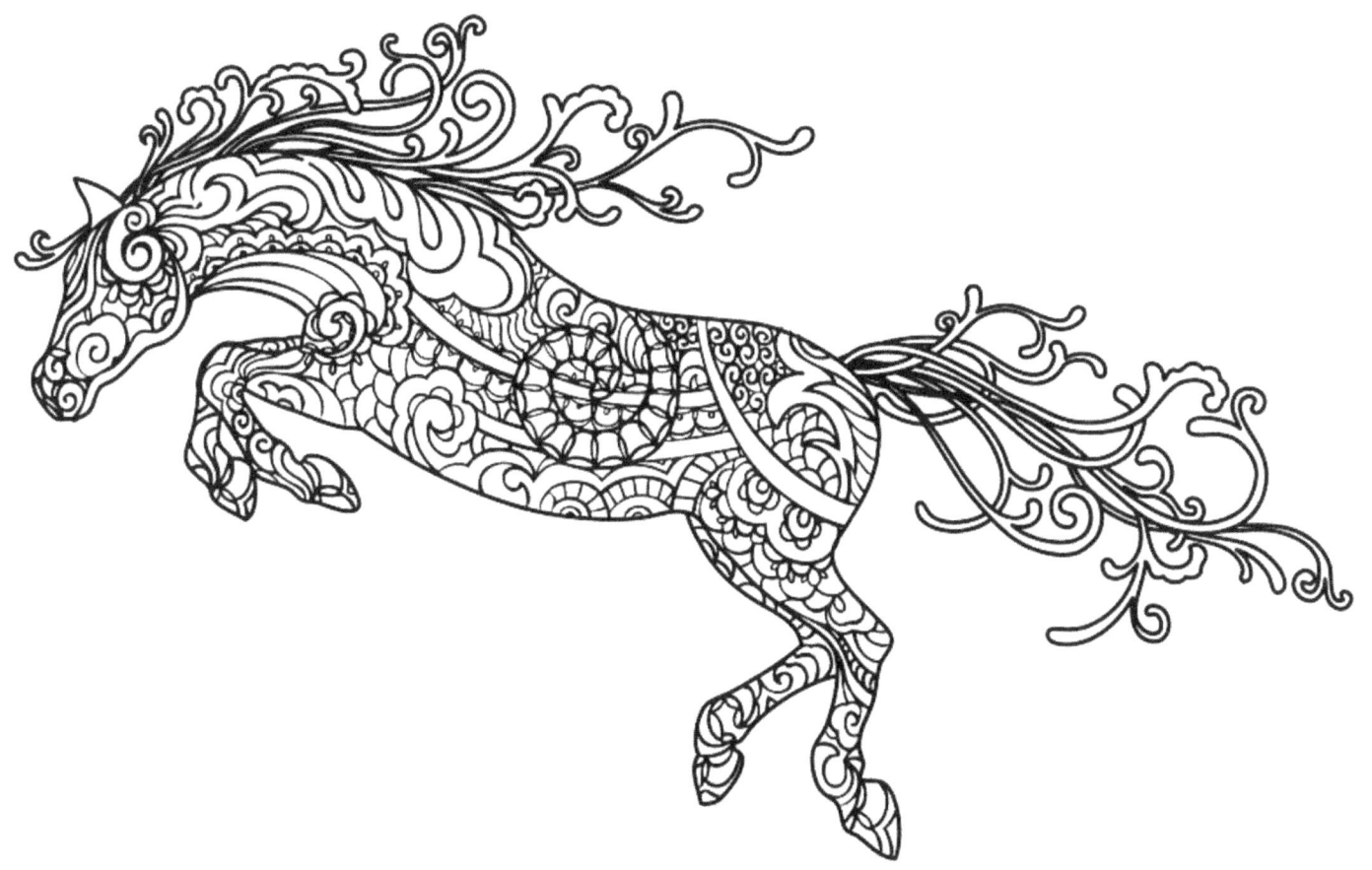

MIXED TATTOO COLORING BOOK

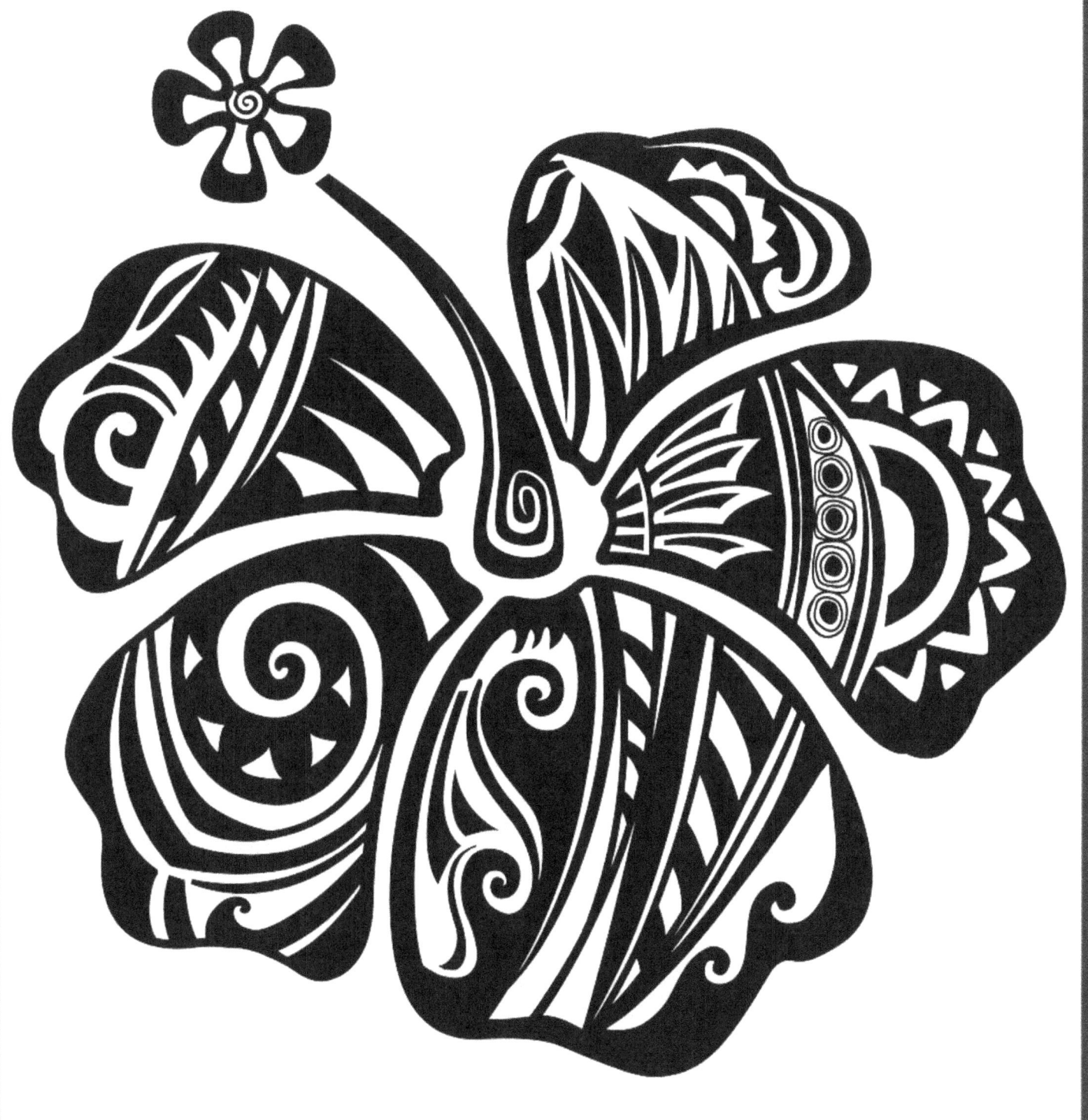

MIXED TATTOO COLORING BOOK

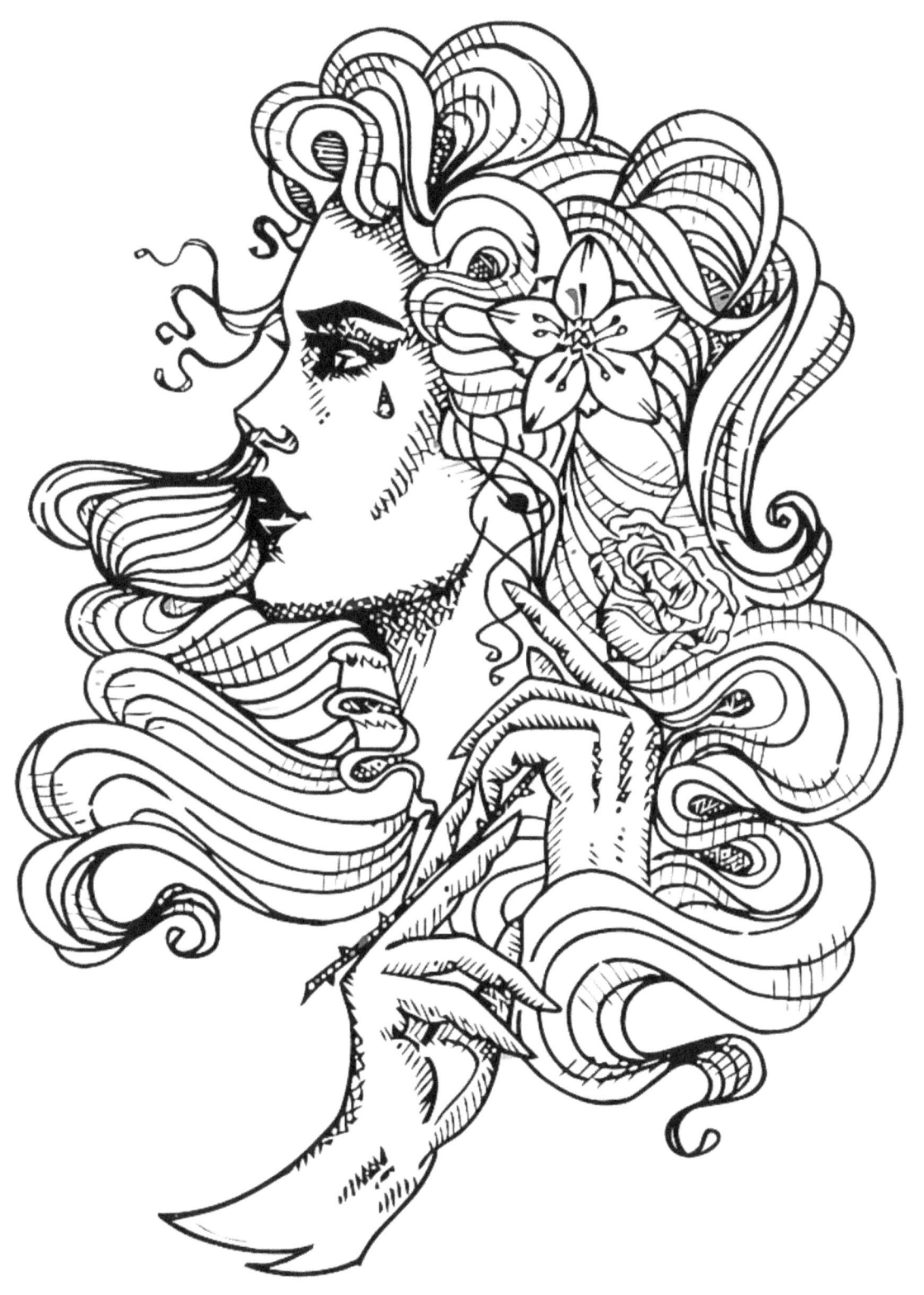

MIXED TATTOO COLORING BOOK

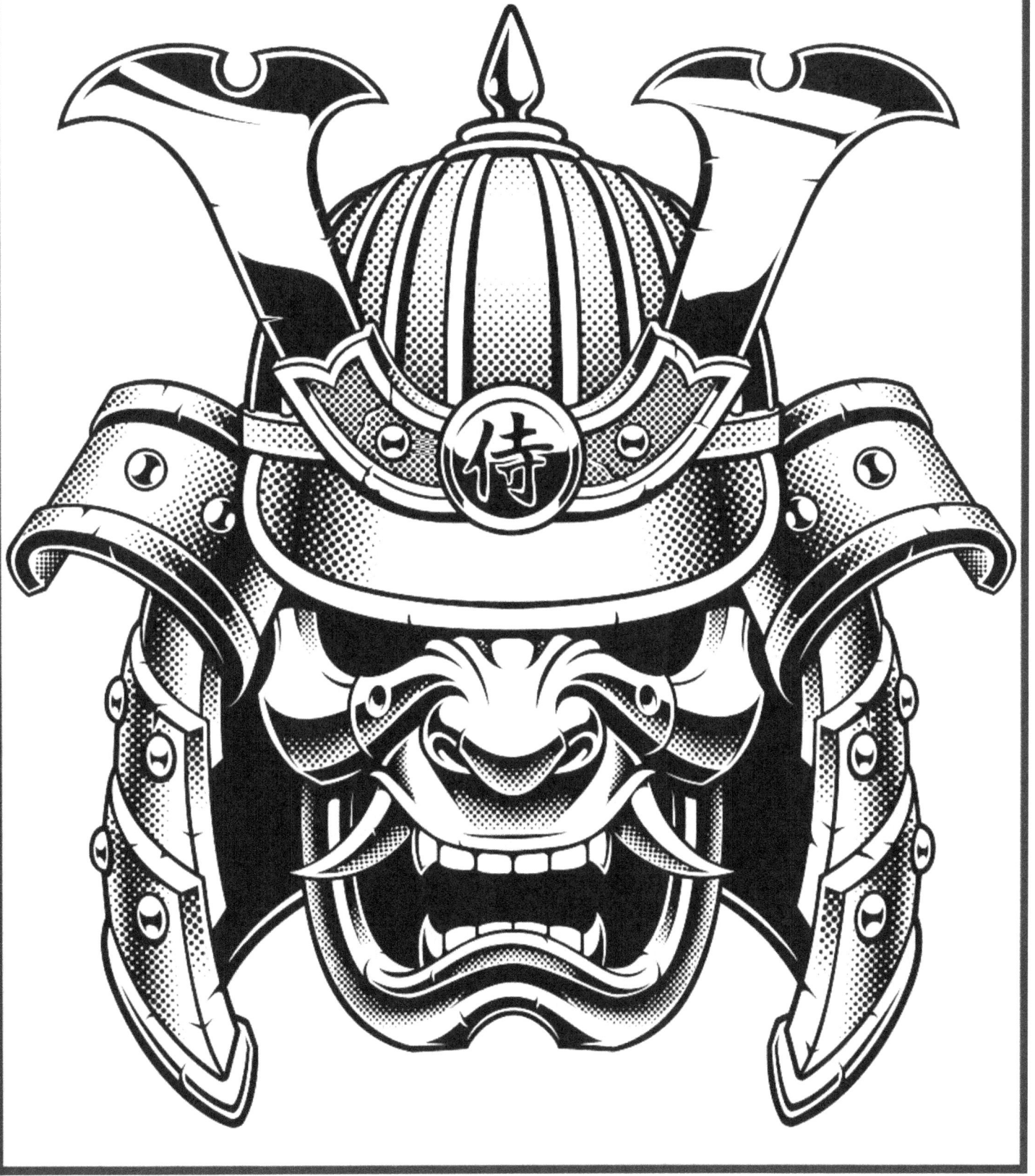

MIXED TATTOO COLORING BOOK

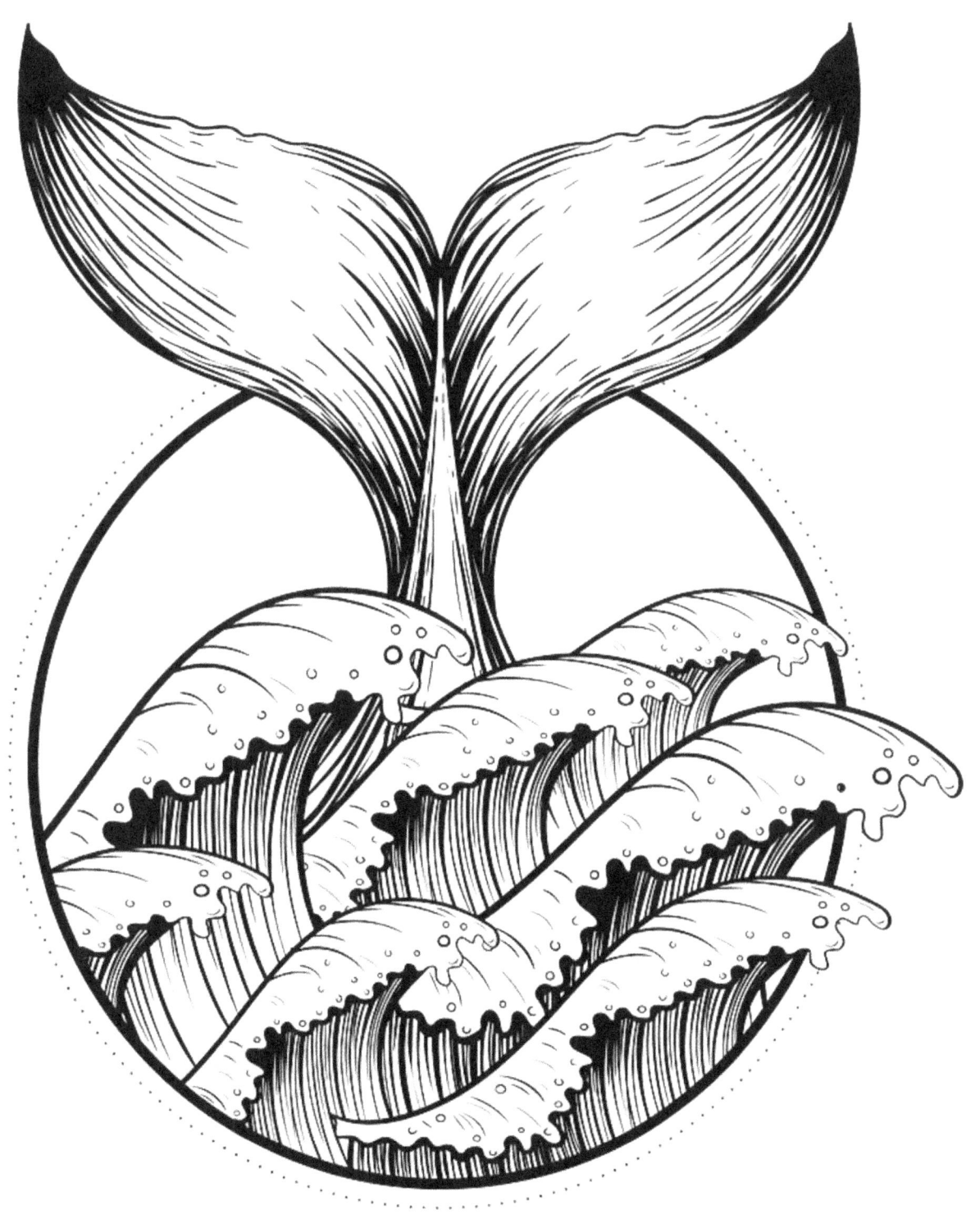

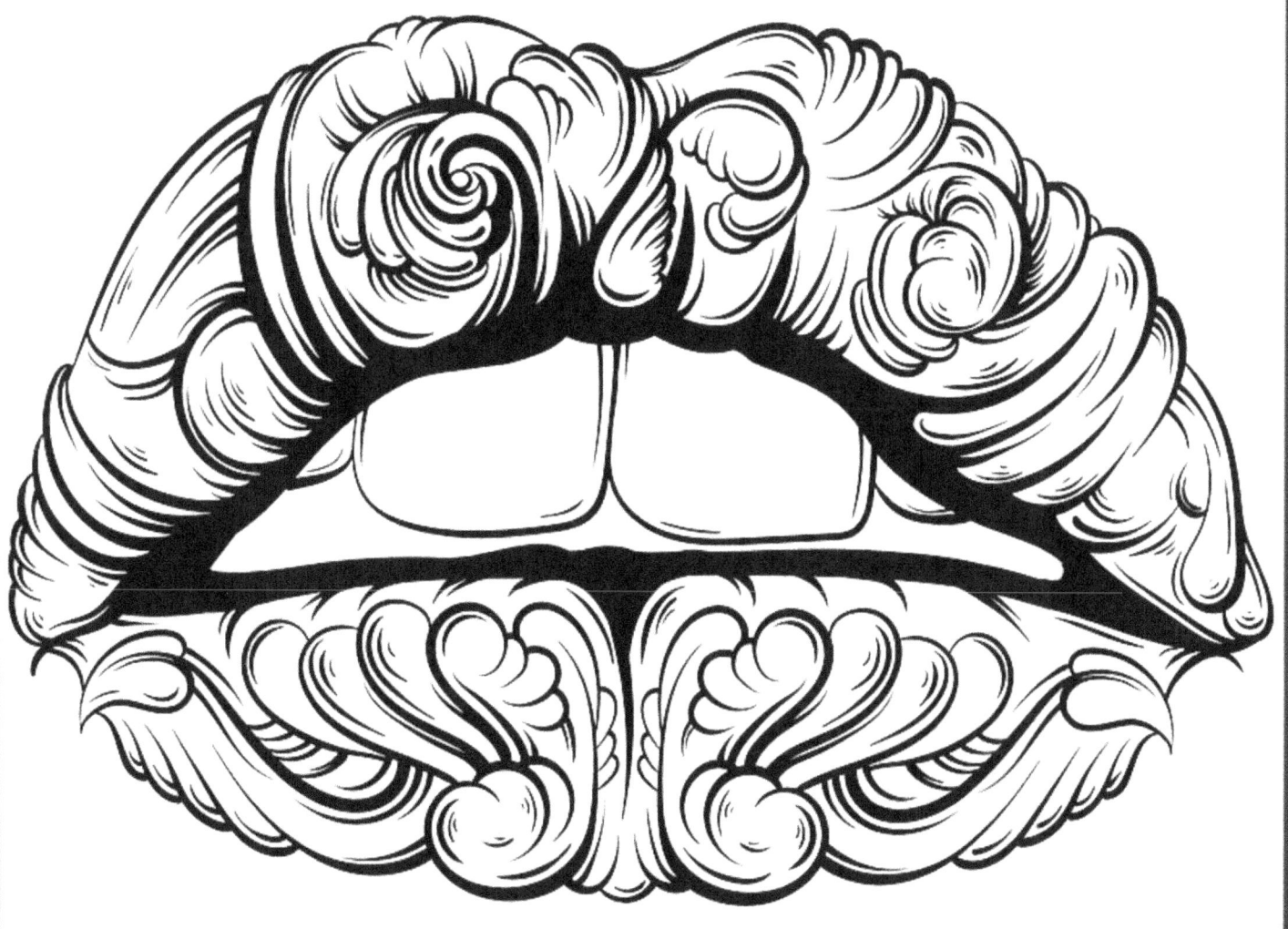

MIXED TATTOO COLORING BOOK

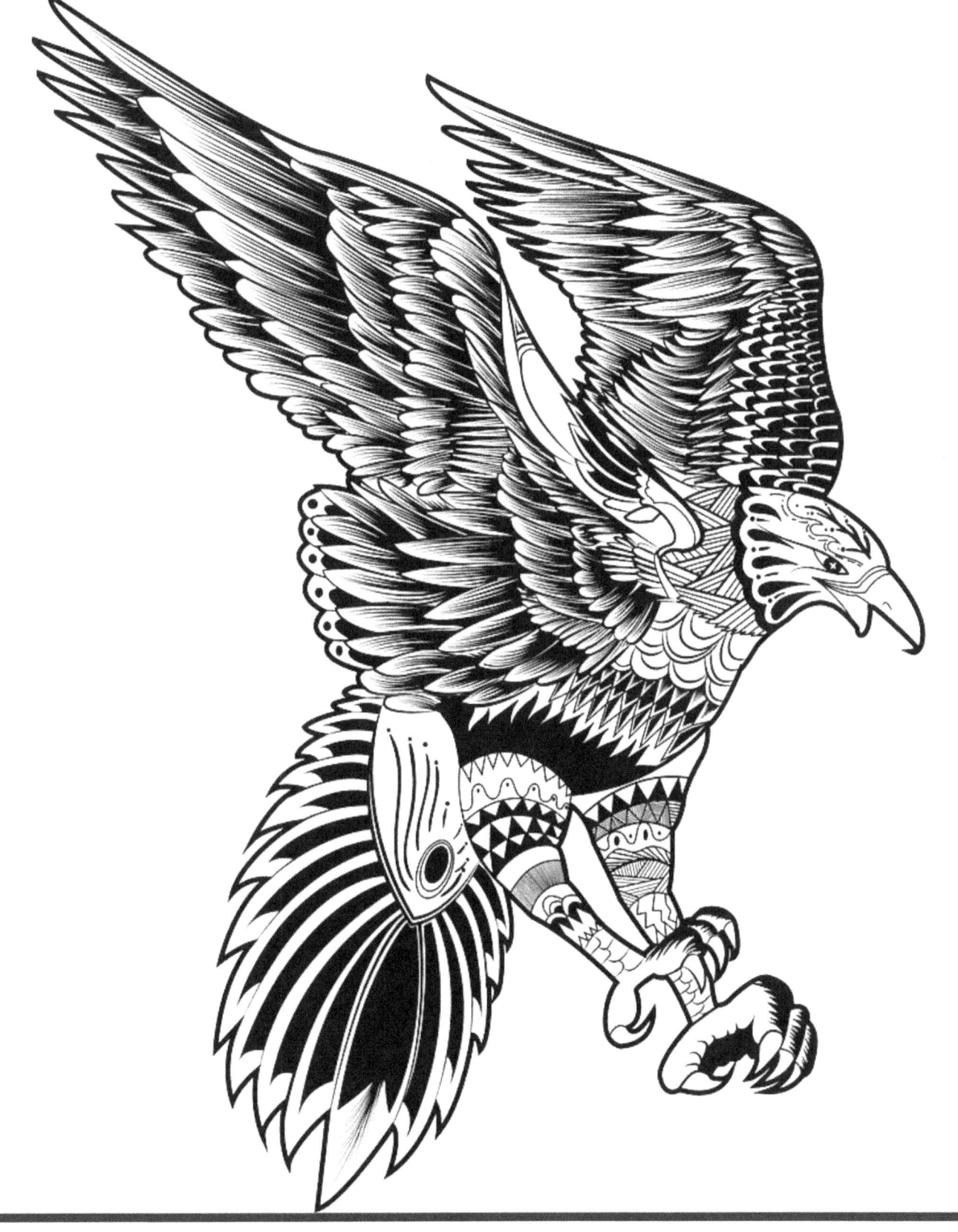

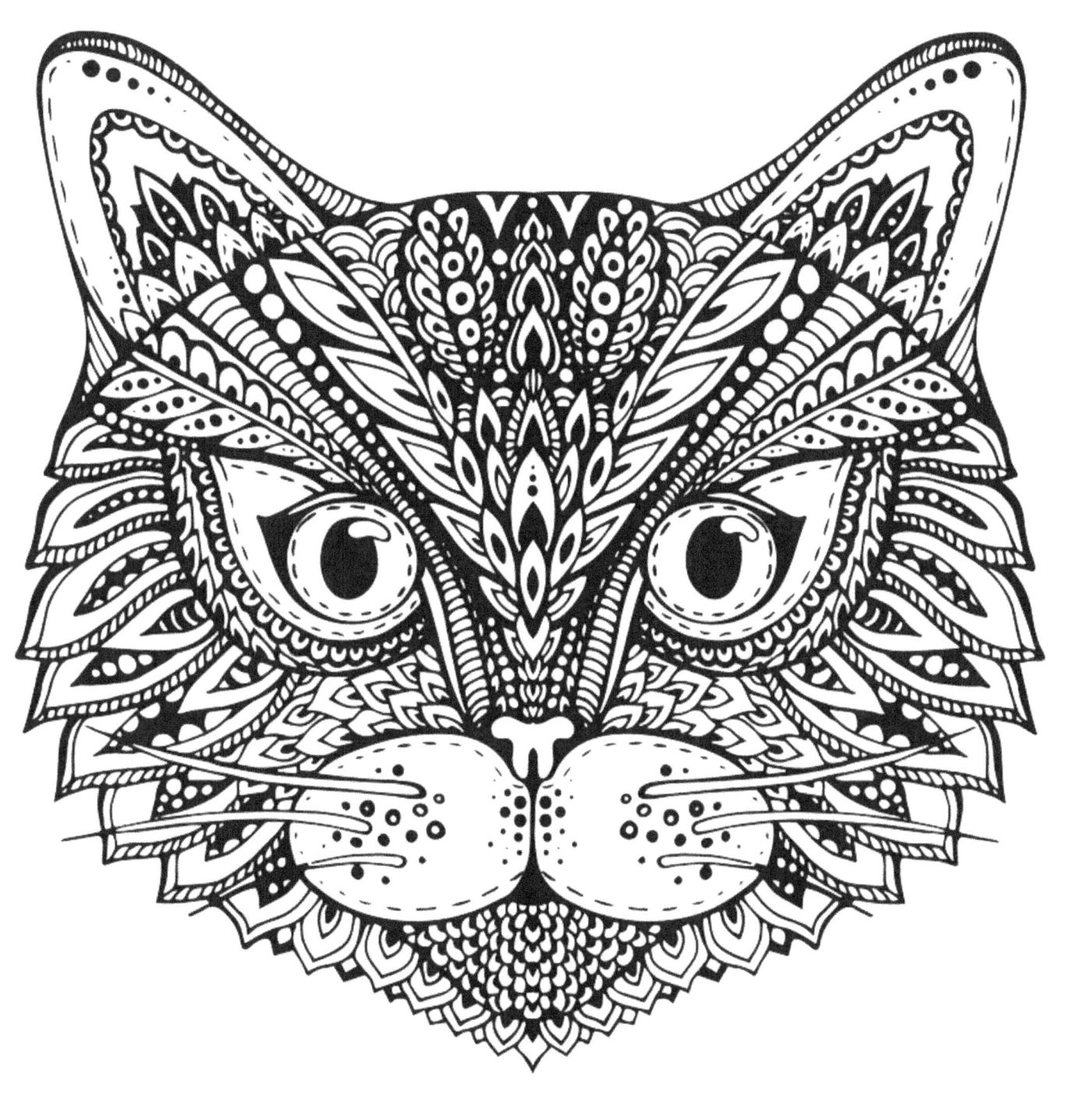

MIXED TATTOO COLORING BOOK

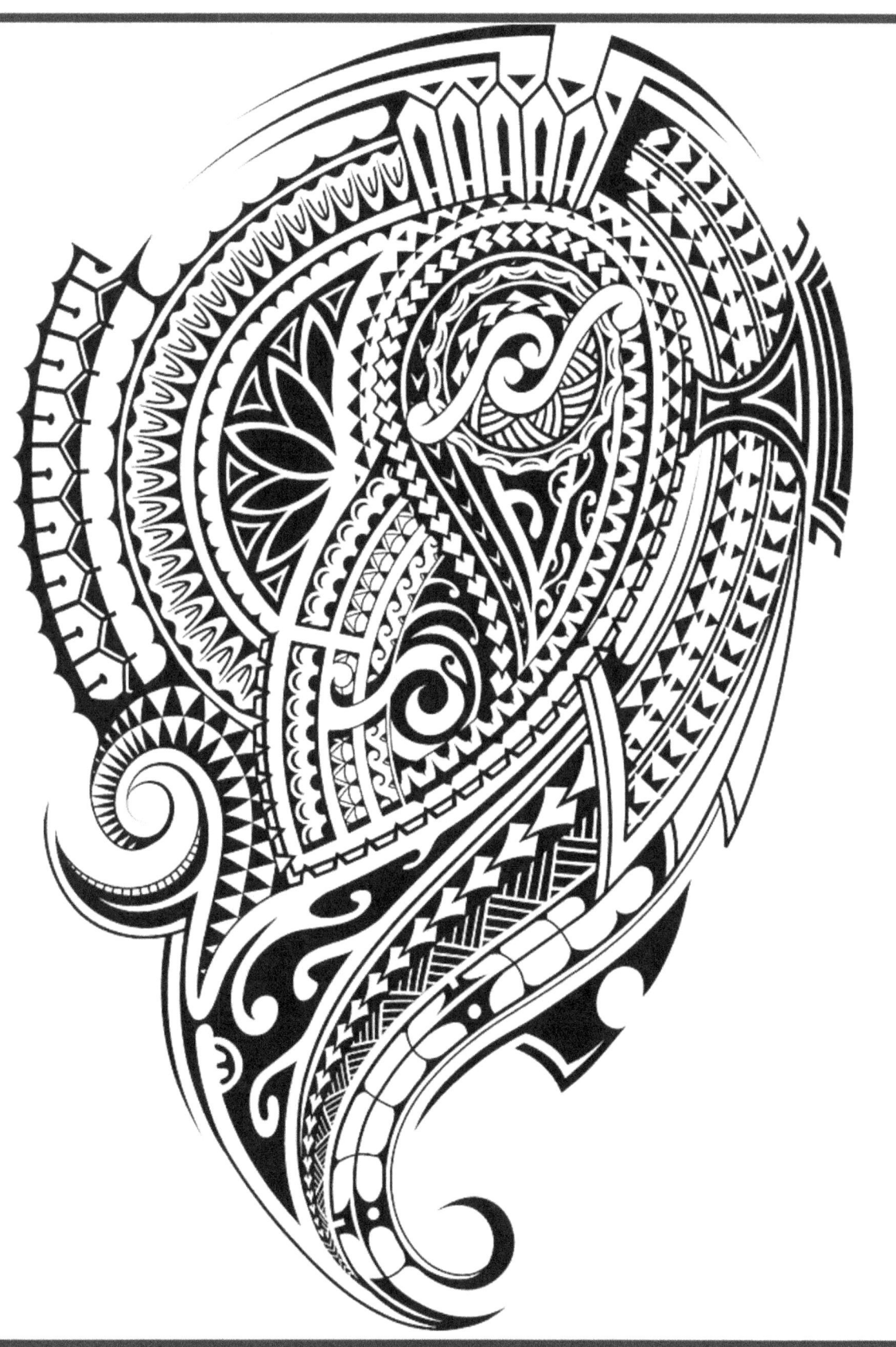

MIXED TATTOO COLORING BOOK

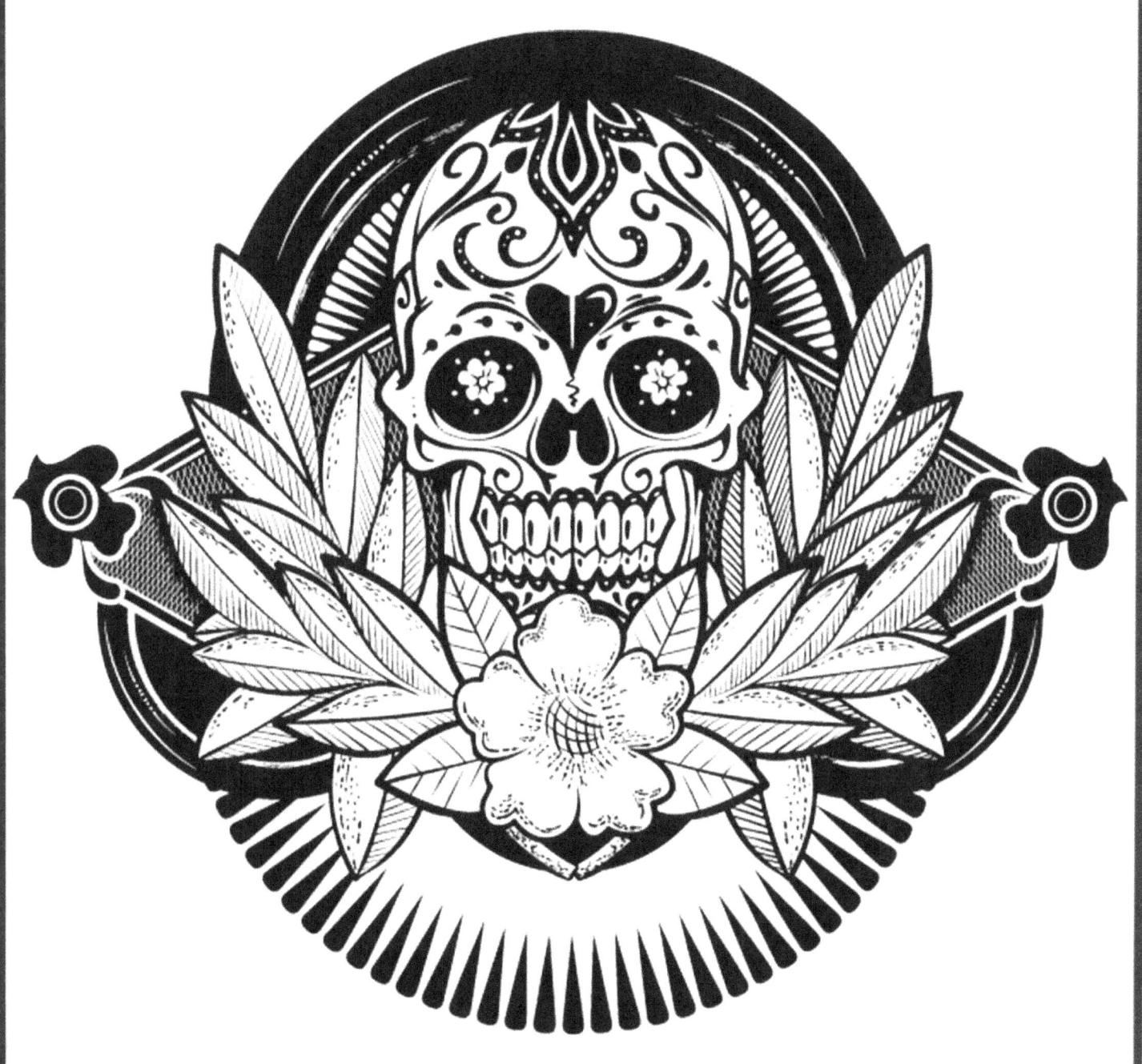

MIXED TATTOO COLORING BOOK

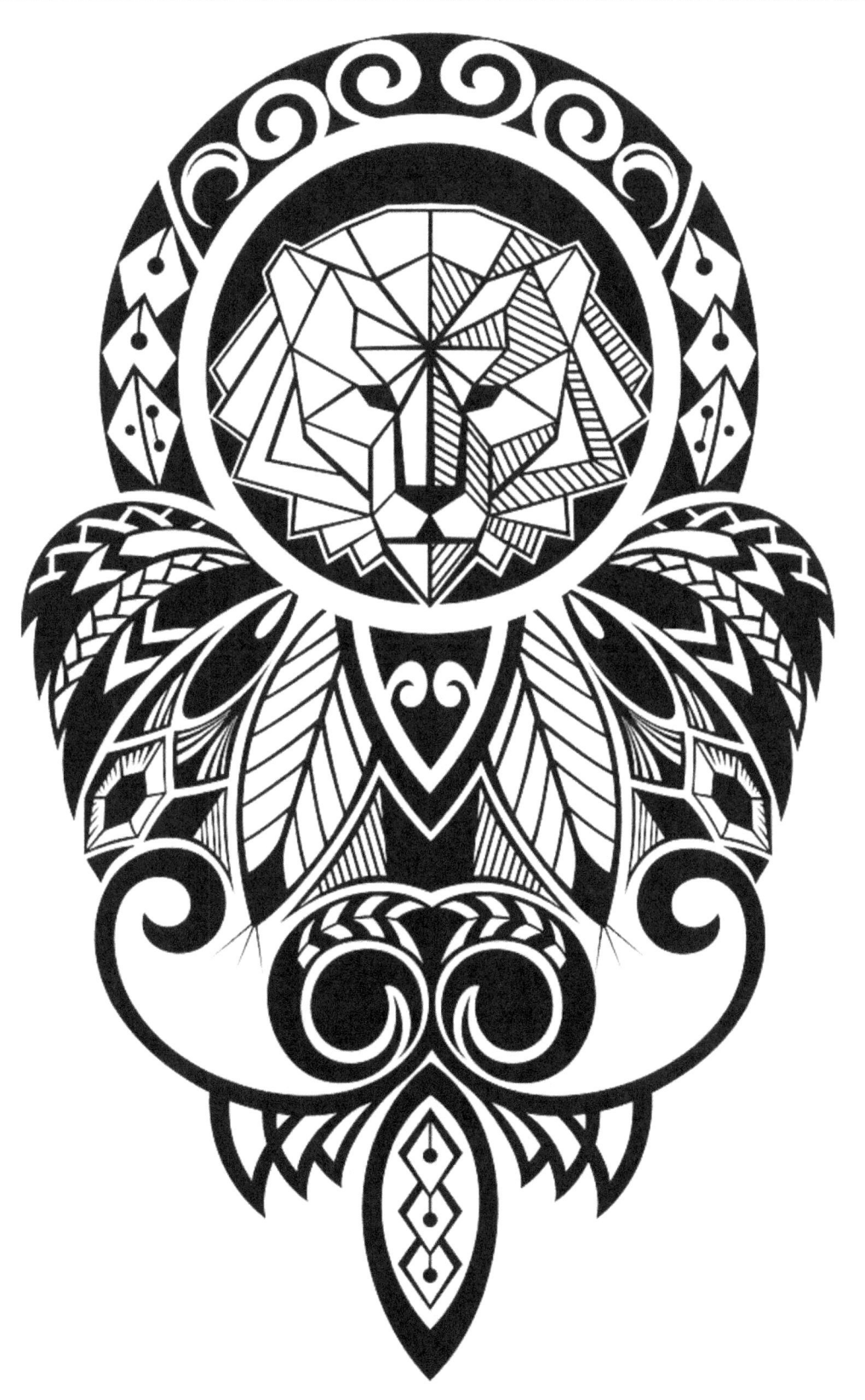

Enjoying this Notebook?

Please leave *Black Rose Press House* a review
because we would love to know your thought,
feedback, and opinions to create
better products for you.
*Please share how you creatively use your
notebooks and journals.*

THANKS
FOR YOUR SUPPORT

Scan This Qr Code And Visit Our
Author Page At-
amazon.com